D1560800

Eddie Merlot's ™

prime aged beef and seafood

prime aged beef and seafood

ISBN 978-0-9713767-1-7

Manufactured in the United States of America
Fort Wayne Printing Company, Inc.

Published by Golden Rock, Inc.
2427 S. Hadley Rd.
Fort Wayne, IN 46804

Front cover photos:
Eddie's Famous Shrimp Cocktail, page 68
Filet Trio of Medallions with Oscar Enhancement, page 120
Pan Fried Crab Cakes, page 72
Carrot Cake, page 192

Back cover photos:
Spinach Salad, page 106
Banana Cream Pie, page 186
New Orleans Mixed Grill, page 124
Lobster Mashed Potatoes, page 162

prime aged beef and seafood

Recipes
Eddie Merlot's chefs and sous chefs,
past and present

General Editors
Margy Hooker and Matthew Nolot

Note Boxes
Matthew Nolot

Photography
Neal Bruns
Tony Frantz
Steve Vorderman
Eric Wagner

Food Styling
Matthew Nolot

Typist
Brooke Branyan

Project Manager and Publisher
Margy Hooker of Golden Rock, Inc.

"The only time to eat diet food is while you're waiting for the steak to cook."

- Julia Child

I would like to personally extend my gratitude to the chefs of Eddie Merlot's, past and present, the sous chefs, and the ladies and gentlemen that make up our culinary team.

Without their sacrifices and hard work ethic, this book would not have been possible and we would not be able to serve the distinguished food that our reputation has been built on and our guests have come to expect.

I would like to extend a special thank you to the opening chef, Jerry Wilson, who was with us in the beginning and provided the great platform for us to reach the new heights we have achieved today.

Lastly, my gratitude and appreciation to Chef Matthew Nolot for his countless hours spent transforming the recipes to be enjoyed in your homes and Margy Hooker, project manager and publisher, whose tireless efforts have made this book a reality.

Tuscan Strip Steak with Tapenade Butter page 128

prime aged beef and seafood

a journey through **taste**
with one of america's
great **steak**
houses

contents

ACKNOWLEDGEMENTS 7

FROM THE CHEF 13
The Quest for Flavor
Their Secrets to Making a Great Steak at Home
Cooking Temperatures for Steak

WINE 18

BASICS 24
Sauces
Stocks
Marinades

APPETIZERS 58

SOUPS 76

SALADS AND DRESSINGS 90

ENTREES 112
Beef, Pork, Veal, Lamb and Game
Poultry
Seafood

SIDES 154

BUTTERS AND SPICES 170
Butters
Spices

DESSERTS 182

THE LOUNGE 202

CELEBRATIONS 212
Wedding Events
Cocktail and Hors d'oeuvre Receptions
Intimate, Holiday and Corporate Events

SOURCE GUIDE 234

INDEX 236

NOTES 239

LOCATIONS 240

Quality Prime Steaks

the quest for flavor

The modern steak house is using very different beef compared to what cattle ranchers provided up to the 1950s and the 1960s. Declining beef sales due to health concerns led ranchers to raise leaner cattle, which were bred with larger and leaner European cattle. Ultimately, this resulted in bigger and leaner steaks. Over time this has resulted in beef with considerably less intramuscular fat, also known as marbling. More marbling translates to more flavor and a higher USDA grade.

Only 2% of beef today is awarded the highest U.S.D.A. grade, Prime. Most of which is sold to buyers from Japan, which leaves very little for the high-end steak house tables like Eddie Merlot's. About 45% of beef is graded Choice and 21% are stamped with the grade, Select which has only 2/3 of the marbling as Prime.

Since only the top 2 grades, Prime and Choice, demand a premium price to justify the cost of voluntary grading; meat packers choose to pay to have their meat graded for quality. Many packers instruct the inspectors not to bother grading beef that are not Prime or Choice. This ungraded meat is called No Roll because the rolling stamp of the inspector is not applied to the carcass. Most of the beef in supermarkets is sold as this.

It is well worth the effort to find a butcher who will sell Prime beef. Since Prime is so expensive, it is almost always sold as steaks and roasts. So you won't see tougher cuts advertised as Prime. If you find a butcher who deals in Prime beef and cuts up their own carcasses, see if they will sell you some of the tougher cuts, such as short ribs or chuck. They will be extra juicy with a great, beefy flavor.

from the chefs

their secrets to making a great steak at home

Bryan Hopping - Cincinnati, Ohio

Bryan's interest in cooking was sparked at age 10, when his family moved to Germany. After earning a bachelor's degree in environmental studies and geology at Middlebury College in Vermont, Bryan decided to pursue a culinary career. He brings to Eddie Merlot's his knowledge of world cuisines from his extensive travels in Europe and Asia. When he's not in the kitchen, Bryan loves to spend time with his wife and two children.

"When cooking a steak either at home or the restaurant I always start with the best quality beef I can find. I love a steak with a good crust and a ton of flavor. I like to make a spice rub that I apply to the steak a little before cooking. You can use any spices you like; personally I use bold earthy spices like cumin, coriander, Garam Marsala, and mustard seeds. Use toasted whole spices and crust them with a mortar and pestle. I've found that a pizza rock or brick wrapped in foil and heated in a hot oven allows me to get a nice crust on the steak and not smoke up the house too much."

Geoff Kelty - Columbus, Ohio

Geoff's father was a certified pastry chef and culinary educator. So as long as he can remember, he's been decorating and delivering cakes, pastries and pies. While a student at Ivy Tech Community College, Geoff studied for three summers throughout Europe. He earned a double major in culinary arts and baking and pastry arts, then served as an instructor before coming to Eddie's. You can find Geoff playing volleyball, golf, Texas Hold'em and target shooting.

"There is no secret to enjoying a great grilled steak. First and foremost, choose a great quality steak from the butcher shop. The cut of steak usually depends on one's personal taste and preference (if you prefer tender, go for a filet mignon; if more marbling is preferred, go with a strip or ribeye). Season your desired steak with kosher salt and black pepper and sear on a high heat grill in order to seal in the juices inside the steak. Cook your steak to the desired temperature and enjoy. It is important to first master this skill, and then go in to adding different flavor profiles and techniques."

their secrets to making a great steak at home

Matt Nolot - Fort Wayne, Indiana

Matt joined Eddie's in 2003 and brings more than 25 years' experience to bear on his work in the kitchen. He's won regional and national cooking competitions and contributed to local and national magazine articles. Matt has a passion for anything pork-related and spice, and he loves traveling for new culinary experiences.

"For grilling at home, some chefs swear by technique, how hot a fire, how many minutes to cook, what type of fuel to use. For other chefs it's all about the quality of the raw ingredients; the highest quality aged beef you can afford, sea salt from France or Olive oil from Italy. To others it's all about the flavor and aroma. Taste and texture are their biggest considerations.

I believe in all of these factors. But the main question I'll be asking after grilling is 'was it fun?' Because in my mind that's the most crucial part of any food experience.

That's why I love to grill at home, it makes me smile. It makes me laugh and I love hanging out with people and doing it. Grilling should be a release, not a chore, which means that at all costs it should be approached in a laid back, light hearted direction. The fun is in the cooking, eating and being with the people you love, not the perfection of the craft."

Reid Craig - Indianapolis, Indiana

Reid is the Executive Chef of the Eddie Merlot's location in Indianapolis. Reid landed his first restaurant job at the age of 13, serving as a dishwasher, and worked his way up to sous chef by the age of 17. He earned a Bachelor of Science in Business and International Business from Indiana University in Indianapolis in August 2004.

Reid worked at several fine dining restaurants in Indianapolis before he was hired by Eddie Merlot's as sous chef, staying for two years, leaving to open his own restaurant, L.A. Café. After that restaurant closed, he returned to Eddie Merlot's in 2010 as sous chef, and was promoted to Executive Chef in 2011.

"I believe there are five key elements in cooking a great steak. Grade of steak, the right seasoning, a medium grill temperature, flavored lava rocks or wood chips, and a great wine to pair with (or liquor if you prefer). Each one of these elements has to meet your standards before one can be even satisfied with the desired illumination of beef. I prefer a thick cut of Kobe beef grilled with blackening seasoning and lava salt on a low temperature non-gas grill with freshly cut apple wood chips followed with a nice glass of Woodford Reserve with a splash of coke!"

from the chefs

cooking temperatures for steak

Blue rare or very rare —
cooked very quickly; the outside is seared, but the inside is usually cool and barely cooked. The steak will be red on the inside and barely warmed; this is also sometimes referred to as 'Black and Blue' or 'Pittsburgh Rare'.

Rare — (110 °F core temperature)
the outside is grey-brown, and the middle of the steak is red and slightly warm.

Medium rare — (120 °F core temperature)
the steak will have a fully red, warm center. This is the standard degree of cooking at most steakhouses, unless specified otherwise.

Medium — (130 °F core temperature)
the middle of the steak is hot and red with pink surrounding the center. The outside is grey-brown.

Medium well done — (140 °F core temperature)
the meat is light pink surrounding the center.

Well done — (150 °F and above core temperature)
the meat is grey-brown throughout and slightly charred.

Overcook — (160 °F core temperature)
the meat is dark throughout and slightly bitter.

The common denominator among the chefs to making a great steak at home is to start with a great quality of meat and then add your preferred seasonings.

Wine Spectator gives all Eddie Merlot's its Award of Excellence

Eddie Merlot's has earned Wine Spectator's Award of Excellence for the 10th straight year. It's our most coveted designation, and one we're proud to have earned every year since we opened in 2001.

Part of what makes us a terrific choice is the range of selection. We have unusually large wine storage racks that display all of the choices available. We serve over 75 wines by the glass-representing wine makers from the world's best growing areas. Our Reserve lists offer over 150 selections, assurance that you will find the perfect selection to complement your meal.

We believe in de-mystifying wine for our clients who do not know their way around wine as well as we do. Our Progressive Wine List is designed to make selecting wines easy for the casual wine drinker and connoisseurs alike. Unlike a traditional list, a well-crafted progressive wine list allows you, as our guest, to easily navigate your way through flavor types and features to find the most appropriate choice for you and your guests. It also allows our service team to help select the perfect wine for your occasion and full enjoyment. All of our wines on the list are logically listed according to a few simple rules, making it easy to locate specific wines and particular flavors for both you and your guests.

wine

flavor terminology on our wine list

Sweet Wines—

Sweet wines contain residual sugars, giving these wines a very perceptible sweet taste. It is possible for wines without these sugars to appear sweet, simply because of their intense fruitiness. These wines, considered less dry or off dry, are placed in the sweet category as well.

Dry Wines—

Dry wines have little to no residual sugar. They are often higher in tannins, which impart an astringent, sometimes bitter flavor to wines.

Mild Intensity—

These wines have very delicate flavors with no perceptible bitterness.

Medium Intensity—

Slightly more robust than mild wines, these often have more distinct flavors.

Full Intensity—

These strongly flavored wines are often complex and quite intense. Full intensity wines generally have much higher levels of tannins.

Eddie Merlot's™

prime aged beef and seafood

Eddie's Classic Grilled Filet with Merchant De Vin Sauce (Wine Makers Sauce) page 40

the basics

Sauces

Stocks

Marinades

Buttermilk Fried Lobster with Five Cheese Sauce

Steamed Mediterranean Halibut

Kentucky Bourbon Marinated Ribeye

Andouille Sausage Gravy

MAKES 3 CUPS

¼ cup vegetable oil

3 cups andouille sausage, ¼" diced

¼ cup flour

1½ cups yellow onion, chopped

1½ cups celery, chopped

1½ cups green pepper, chopped

2 bay leaves

1 teaspoon dry mustard

½ teaspoon kosher salt

½ teaspoon white pepper

½ teaspoon cayenne pepper

½ teaspoon dried basil leaves

½ teaspoon dried thyme leaves

1 tablespoon garlic, minced

4 cups homemade Beef Stock, page 52

Kosher salt

In a heavy bottom sauce pan, heat the vegetable oil until almost smoking. Carefully add the diced andouille sausage and fry until golden brown on all sides. Remove the sausage pieces from the oil with a slotted spoon and set aside. Whisk the flour into the hot oil; reduce heat to medium and cook roux, stirring constantly until it is deep dark brown, almost red in color. Add the onions, celery and bell peppers and cook for 1 more minute. Add the dry seasonings, the browned andouille sausage, garlic and the beef stock. Bring to a boil, reduce heat to a simmer and cook for 30 minutes. Season with more salt if necessary. Remove bay leaves and keep warm until needed.

This recipe goes with the New Orleans Mixed Grill recipe on page 124.

A Really Good Tartare Sauce

MAKES 1¾ CUPS

1 anchovy fillet

2 tablespoons yellow onion, chopped

1½ tablespoons chopped parsley, stems removed

1 tablespoon capers, drained

1¼ teaspoons black olives, finely chopped

2½ tablespoons dill pickle, finely chopped

1½ cups mayonnaise

3-4 drops Tabasco sauce

3 tablespoons heavy cream

Kosher salt

Black pepper

Place the anchovy fillet, onion, parsley, capers, black olives and pickles in a food processor and pulse until thoroughly chopped. Spoon mixture into a mixing bowl, add the remaining ingredients, season with salt and pepper and mix well. Serve with anything fried, especially fried pickles. Refrigerate any leftovers for up to 7 days.

When researching tartare sauce recipes we set two goals that we wanted to hit. #1 It had to be simple, not too many ingredients that detracted from what a classic tartare sauce is and #2 it had to taste great with every type of fish we offer. This recipe hit our criteria and was actually perfected by our Director of Operations.

Bacon and Gorgonzola Cheese Crust

MAKES 2 CUPS

¼ pound bacon, ½" diced

½ pound gorgonzola cheese, crumbled

¾ teaspoon fresh parsley, chopped

¾ cup Bleu Cheese Dressing, page 108

½ teaspoon Tabasco sauce

½ teaspoon Worcestershire sauce

In a small sauté pan, cook the bacon until all the fat is rendered and the bacon is crispy. Drain and set aside to cool. Mix the rest of the ingredients together in a small mixing bowl. Fold in the cooled crispy bacon and mix well.

This recipe goes with the Filet Trio of Medallions on page 120.

This crust gives unparalleled taste and texture to filet mignons. It is sure to impress even the pickiest filet connoisseur in your family. The only way to make this better is to use an Apple Wood Smoked Bacon. It is about double the price of regular bacon, but the apple wood smoke flavor is a great compliment to the gorgonzola cheese.

New Orleans Mixed Grill with Andouille Sausage Gravy page 26

Basic Tomato-Basil Sauce

MAKES 5 CUPS

4 tablespoons extra virgin olive oil

2 tablespoons garlic, minced

¼ cup yellow onions, minced

4 tablespoons white wine

3 cups tomatoes with juice, crushed

1 tablespoon fresh basil leaves, chopped

1 teaspoon dried oregano leaves

4 tablespoons tomato paste

1 tablespoon sugar

Kosher salt

Black pepper

In a medium sauce pan, heat olive oil over medium heat. Add the garlic and onion and sauté until translucent, stirring often, about 4-5 minutes. Add the white wine and allow mixture to reduce by about half. Add the remaining ingredients, season with salt and pepper and reduce heat to a simmer. Cook sauce for 15 minutes over low heat, stirring occasionally. Store sauce in refrigerator until needed.

Blueberry Jalapeño Barbecue Sauce

MAKES 2 CUPS

2 teaspoons vegetable oil

2 tablespoons shallot, minced

2 teaspoons garlic, minced

1 tablespoon jalapeño, minced

¼ cup ketchup

¼ cup rice vinegar

6 tablespoons brown sugar

2 cups fresh blueberries

½ tablespoon Tabasco sauce

½ teaspoon cumin

½ teaspoon crushed red pepper

1 tablespoon fresh cilantro leaves, chopped

In a small sauce pan, sauté the onions and garlic in vegetable oil over medium heat until soft. Add the rest of the ingredients except the cilantro and bring sauce to a simmer and cook for 15 minutes. Remove from heat and allow to cool slightly before pureeing in a food processor and straining through a fine sieve. Fold in the chopped cilantro. Refrigerate any leftovers for up to 7 days.

This recipe is great served with grilled wild game, venison and elk.

Burgundy Wine Sauce

MAKES 3 CUPS

1 cup burgundy wine

1 fresh rosemary sprig

3-4 fresh thyme sprigs

1 shallot, chopped

1 bay leaf

3 cups Basic Veal Sauce, page 50

Kosher salt

Black pepper

In a small sauce pan, combine the burgundy wine, rosemary, thyme, shallot and bay leaf. Bring mixture to a boil, reduce heat and simmer until there is about ¼ cup of liquid left. Add the Basic Veal Sauce, season with salt and pepper and continue to simmer for 12-15 minutes. Strain through a fine sieve and keep warm until needed.

This sauce is wonderful served with roasted meats such as Chateaubriand and Prime Rib.

Lobster Wellington with Burgundy Wine Sauce page 28

Caramelized Red Onion Jam

MAKES 2 CUPS

9 ounces red onions, julienned

1 tablespoon olive oil

¼ teaspoon kosher salt

2 tablespoons red wine vinegar

2 tablespoons red wine

2 tablespoons brown sugar

2 tablespoons honey

1½ teaspoons grenadine

½ lemon, zested

1½ teaspoons fresh thyme leaves, chopped

¼ teaspoon black pepper

In a medium sauté pan, cook the onions in olive oil with the salt, over medium low heat until a light golden brown color is achieved, stirring frequently. Add the red wine vinegar and the red wine. Cook for 5 more minutes. Add the brown sugar, honey and grenadine; reduce heat to low and cook until mixture reaches syrup consistency. Add the thyme leaves and lemon zest. Store leftovers in the refrigerator. Reheat slightly before using.

This recipe is served with the Blackened Scallops and the Sea Bass at the Eddie Merlot restaurants.

Chimichurri Sauce

MAKES 2 CUPS

2 tablespoons garlic, minced

3 bay leaves

2 large Serrano peppers

2 cups Italian parsley

½ cup fresh oregano

¾ cup white vinegar

¾ cup extra virgin olive oil

3 tablespoons kosher salt

1½ teaspoons black pepper

Coarsely chop the bay leaves, Serrano peppers, Italian parsley and oregano. Place chopped herbs and peppers in a food processor with the rest of the ingredients and pulse several times to combine. Brush over chicken or pork chops during the last 5-6 minutes of cooking or use to marinate chicken or pork chops over night before grilling. Refrigerate any leftovers for up to 3 days.

This sauce goes with the Chimichurri Pork Chops with Pineapple Salsa, page 116.

Chipotle Grilling Sauce

MAKES 2 CUPS

1 7- ounce can chipotle peppers in adobo sauce

1½ cups extra virgin olive oil

3 tablespoons cilantro, chopped

2 tablespoons garlic, minced

3 limes, juiced

2 tablespoons honey

Kosher salt

Black pepper

Place all ingredients into a food processor, season with salt and pepper and pulse until well combined. Use to brush on chicken, salmon or pork chops during the last 6-7 minutes of cooking.

For an over the top recipe, finish your meat with the Chipotle Butter on page 172.

Chimichurri is a simple steak sauce that originated from Argentina. With just a few simple ingredients and a couple hours of marinating time, this recipe will add a kick of flavor to any cut of beef, pork or chicken. It will have everyone asking you where you got the recipe.

We created this recipe for our widely popular Summer Grill Promotion that we do on an annual basis. It is a quick sauce that has a smoky and sweet bite that only chipotles can deliver.

Maple and Apple Cider Glazed Seabass with Caramelized Red Onion Jam page 30

Cinnamon and Clove Spiced Moroccan Ketchup

MAKES 3 CUPS

2   tablespoons ginger, peeled and minced

1½ tablespoons garlic, minced

1   tablespoon shallot, minced

3   tablespoons olive oil

5   tablespoons cider vinegar

2   cinnamon sticks

½   cup brown sugar

2½ cups tomatoes, finely chopped

½   teaspoon cayenne pepper

¼   teaspoon ground cloves

⅓   cup honey

Kosher salt

Black pepper

In a medium sauce pan, sauté ginger, garlic and shallots in olive oil until soft, about 3-4 minutes. Add the cider vinegar and the cinnamon sticks and reduce liquid by half. Add the brown sugar, tomatoes, cayenne pepper and the cloves. Simmer mixture for one hour. Strain through a medium strainer and transfer mixture to a food processor. Season with salt and pepper and puree mixture with the honey for 2 minutes until completely smooth. Allow to cool to room temperature before using

This ketchup makes a nice glaze for grilled chicken breasts and is also great on a grilled lamb pita with cucumbers.

Creamed Horseradish Sauce

MAKES 2 CUPS

1¼ cups sour cream

2   teaspoons Worcestershire sauce

¾   teaspoon Tabasco sauce

½   cup fresh horseradish, grated

½   fresh lemon, juiced

¼   cup heavy cream

2   teaspoons parsley, chopped

Kosher salt

Black pepper

Combine all ingredients together in a mixing bowl. Liberally season with salt and pepper and mix well. Store in refrigerator until needed.

Great with prime rib!

We use freshly grated horseradish at the restaurant for all of our recipes. Freshly grated has a sweeter and cleaner taste. If you have any left over, store it in a container filled with a mixture of half water and half vinegar with a tight fitting lid in the refrigerator. When needed, just squeeze out the liquid with your hands before using.

Creamy Wasabi Sauce

MAKES 2 CUPS

2½ tablespoons wasabi powder

1¼ cups mayonnaise

½   cup sour cream

2½ tablespoons honey

2½ tablespoons heavy cream

Kosher salt

White pepper

Combine all ingredients into a food processor, season with salt and pepper and puree until smooth, about 2-3 minutes. Keep refrigerated until needed.

This sauce goes with the Tempura Green Bean recipe, page 74.

Most wasabi powders are just a blend of powdered mustard/horseradish and some green food dye. The fresh root is very expensive and not nearly as harsh as the manufactured product. That doesn't mean it isn't good. It just means we need to use it as a flavor enhancer with other ingredients. Here we mix it with a creamy blend of mayonnaise, sour cream and a touch of honey to smooth it out. It is one of our most popularly requested recipes.

Tempura Green Beans with Wasabi Sauce page 32

Eddie's Homemade Apple Butter

MAKES 6 CUPS

8 cups fresh apple cider

4 pounds Granny Smith apples, quartered, not peeled or cored

½ cup sugar

½ cup corn syrup

1 teaspoon cinnamon

½ teaspoon nutmeg

¼ teaspoon kosher salt

In a large soup pan, bring the apple cider to a boil and allow to reduce by half. Add the apples, reduce heat to low and allow to simmer for 2½ hours. Add the rest of the ingredients and continue to cook for another hour, stirring often. Allow mixture to cool slightly and strain through a fine strainer. Puree until smooth in a food processor. Taste and add more sugar if a sweeter taste is desired. If consistency seems a little thin, place mixture back on the stove over low heat and cook until thickened. Refrigerate until needed.

This apple butter goes great with pork chops and is in our Apple and Peach Crisp recipe on page 184.

Eddie's Homemade Mayonnaise

MAKES 2 CUPS

1 large egg yolk

1½ cups vegetable oil

1 tablespoon cider vinegar

½ teaspoon Tabasco sauce

½ teaspoon kosher salt

½ teaspoon white pepper

Place the egg yolk in a food processor and blend on high for about 30 seconds. With the machine running, slowly add the vegetable oil in a thin, steady stream. When mixture is thick and creamy, add the vinegar, Tabasco, salt and pepper and continue to process for another minute. Refrigerate mayonnaise for about an hour to thicken before using.

Variation: Garlic Mayonnaise

2 tablespoons garlic, minced

2 tablespoons butter, unsalted

2 tablespoons onion, minced

2 tablespoons celery, minced

1 tablespoon fresh lemon juice

In a sauté pan, combine all the ingredients and cook over low heat for about 8-10 minutes or until vegetables are very soft. Remove vegetables from heat and allow to cool to room temperature. Follow the homemade mayonnaise recipe but add the vegetable mixture in with the egg yolk.

Eddie's Shrimp Cocktail Sauce

MAKES 4 CUPS

1¾ cups ketchup

1¼ cups chili sauce

1 tablespoon fresh lemon juice

1½ teaspoon Tabasco sauce

1½ teaspoon Worcestershire sauce

½ teaspoon dry mustard

½ teaspoon kosher salt

Pinch white pepper

Pinch cayenne pepper

1 cup fresh horseradish, grated

Thoroughly mix all ingredients together except the horseradish and keep refrigerated until needed. Right before serving fold in the horseradish and serve immediately.

Oyster Shooters with Eddie's Shrimp Cocktail Sauce page 34

Five Cheese
Mac'n'Cheese Sauce

MAKES 4-6 SERVINGS

2 cups Half & Half

6 ounces mascarpone cheese

4 ounces pepper jack cheese, shredded

2½ ounces Gruyere cheese, shredded

6 ounces cream cheese

2½ ounces Cheddar cheese, shredded

2 teaspoons salt

Pinch white pepper

In a sauce pan, add Half & Half and heat over medium heat. When hot, add the rest of the ingredients and reduce heat to low. Cook over low heat, stirring often until sauce is smooth and thickened. Remove from heat and keep warm.

Garlic-Ginger
Dipping Sauce

MAKES 2 CUPS

¼ cup teriyaki sauce

¼ cup soy sauce

1 cup water

2 teaspoons sherry wine

2½ tablespoons honey

2½ tablespoons brown sugar

1 tablespoon fresh ginger, peeled and minced

4 teaspoons rice vinegar

2 teaspoons sesame oil

¾ teaspoon garlic, minced

½ teaspoon crushed red pepper

Slurry

2 teaspoons corn starch

2 teaspoons water

In a sauce pan mix all of the sauce ingredients together (except slurry) and bring to a simmer over medium heat. In a small bowl whisk the slurry ingredients together, cornstarch and water, until smooth. Slowly whisk the slurry into the simmering sauce. Allow sauce to return to a simmer and cook for about 10 more minutes. Remove from heat and allow to cool before using. Store in the refrigerator until needed.

Hoisin
Barbecue Sauce

MAKES 2 CUPS

10 tablespoons sugar

2 tablespoons water

¾ cup hoisin sauce

¼ cup rice vinegar

1½ tablespoon fish sauce

1½ tablespoon soy sauce

1½ tablespoon honey

1 teaspoon shallots, minced

1 teaspoon fresh ginger, peeled and minced

1 teaspoon garlic, minced

2 teaspoons Sriracha chile sauce

In a mixing bowl, whisk all the ingredients together, except the sugar and water, until smooth. Combine the sugar and water in a heavy, dry sauce pan over medium heat until the sugar starts to melt. Stir mixture with a wooden spoon until sugar is fully melted and cooked to a deep golden brown. Carefully pour in the rest of the ingredients. Mixture will boil rapidly and then settle down. Reduce heat to medium low and cook, stirring often, until caramel is dissolved and sauce is thickened and completely smooth, about 5-6 minutes. Turn off heat and allow to cool before handling. Store in the refrigerator until needed.

Fish sauce is made from fish that are fermented. It is a staple in many cultures in southeast Asia and tastes a lot better than it sounds. It gives a complex saltiness that can be described as Unami, the fifth sense of taste. Fish sauce can be used instead of salt in Asian recipes.

Hoisin Barbecue Chicken Wings page 36

Hollandaise Sauce

MAKES 1⅓ CUPS

1 cup Clarified Butter, page 172

1 large egg yolk

2 tablespoons water

1 tablespoon fresh lemon juice

¾ teaspoon Worcestershire sauce

¼ teaspoon Tabasco sauce

Pinch white pepper

¼ teaspoon kosher salt

Gently warm the Clarified Butter to 155 degrees. While the butter is heating, add the rest of the ingredients to a food processor and process on high for 1 minute. With the motor running, slowly add the hot Clarified Butter in a thin and continuous stream and continue to process for another minute. Taste and season with salt and pepper if necessary. Serve immediately. Discard any leftovers.

Homemade Worcestershire Sauce

MAKES 2 CUPS

1 tablespoon olive oil

¼ cup onion, chopped

1 tablespoon garlic, minced

1 tablespoon fresh ginger root, minced

½ jalapeño, minced

1 tablespoon anchovy, chopped

2 tablespoons tomato paste

2 whole cloves

1 tablespoon black pepper

¼ cup dark corn syrup

½ cup molasses

1½ cups white vinegar

6 ounces dark beer, your favorite

¼ cup orange juice

1 cup water

1 lemon, thinly sliced

1 lime, thinly sliced

Kosher salt

In a medium sauce pan, sauté the onion in the olive oil until a light golden brown, about 7-8 minutes. Add the garlic, ginger and jalapeño and continue to cook over medium heat for another 5 minutes, stirring frequently. Add the rest of the ingredients and bring to a boil. Reduce heat to a simmer and cook until sauce is reduced by half. Season with salt, if needed. Strain sauce through a fine mesh strainer and store in the refrigerator until needed.

Lemon and Roasted Garlic Aioli

MAKES 1 CUP

1 cup mayonnaise

1 tablespoon roasted garlic puree

1 teaspoon fresh rosemary, minced

1 teaspoon fresh lemon juice

1 teaspoon fresh lemon zest

2 teaspoons fresh chives, chopped

Kosher salt

Black pepper

Place all ingredients in a food processor and puree on high until completely smooth, about 1 minute. Season with salt and pepper and pulse to combine. Transfer to a serving container and place in the refrigerator for at least an hour to allow flavors to develop before serving.

This recipe goes great with salmon.

Cedar Plank Salmon with Lemon and Roasted Garlic Aioli page 38

Merchant De Vin Sauce (Wine Makers Sauce)

MAKES 2 CUPS

1   tablespoon olive oil

4   ounces prosciutto ham, minced

6   tablespoons shallots, minced

1½ tablespoon garlic, minced

⅔   cup button mushrooms, minced

½   cup burgundy wine

1½ cups Basic Veal Sauce, page 50

½   teaspoon fresh rosemary, chopped

½   teaspoon fresh thyme, chopped

Kosher salt

Black pepper

In a medium sauce pan, sauté the ham in the olive oil until crispy. Add the garlic, shallots and mushrooms and continue to cook until soft. Drain any grease from the pan. Deglaze pan with the burgundy and allow liquid to boil until the pan is almost dry. Add the Basic Veal Sauce and heat to a simmer. Stir in the chopped herbs and season with salt and pepper and allow to simmer for 7-8 minutes. Skim any oil from the top and enjoy. Refrigerate any leftovers for up to 7 days.

This is a wonderful sauce for any grilled steak.

Peppercorn and Brandy Sauce

MAKES 2 ⅓ CUPS

⅓   cup whole black peppercorns

⅔   cup brandy

1⅓ cups heavy cream

1⅓ cups Basic Veal Sauce, page 50

Kosher salt

Place the peppercorns in a heavy, resealable bag and, using either a mallet or the bottom of a heavy sauce pan, pound the peppercorns so they are cracked, but still in large pieces. In a dry, heavy-bottomed sauce pan toast the peppercorns over medium heat, tossing constantly until fragrant, about 4 minutes. Carefully add the brandy, bring to a boil, reduce heat to a simmer and reduce liquid by 75%. Add heavy cream, raise heat slightly and continue to cook until sauce is reduced by 50%. Add the Basic Veal Sauce and bring to a simmer. Season with salt and keep warm until needed.

Red Ginger-Soy Vinaigrette

MAKES 3 CUPS

1   tablespoon Dijon mustard

½   cup rice wine vinegar

¾   cup soy sauce

3   tablespoons honey

4   tablespoons sesame oil

2   tablespoons sugar

1   teaspoon crushed red pepper

1   cup vegetable oil

4   tablespoons shallot, minced

3   tablespoons pickled ginger, minced

1½ tablespoons garlic, minced

1   tablespoon jalapeño, seeded, minced

Combine the mustard, rice vinegar, soy sauce, honey, sesame oil, sugar and crushed red pepper in a food processor. Puree until smooth. With the motor running, slowly drizzle in the vegetable oil. Add the shallots, pickled ginger and jalapeño and pulse 5-6 times until coarsely chopped. Store in the refrigerator until ready to use.

This vinaigrette is a perfect accompaniment to grilled tuna.

Steak au Poivre with Peppercorn and Brandy Sauce page 40

Red Wine
Mignonette Sauce

MAKES ¾ CUP

⅓ cup dry red wine

⅓ cup red wine vinegar

3 tablespoons cracked black pepper

3 tablespoons shallots, minced

¼ teaspoon kosher salt

Whisk all ingredients together and serve well-chilled with oysters on the half shell.

Mignonette sauce is a classic sauce to serve with raw oysters on the half shell. For many it is the only sauce that should ever touch an oyster. The peppercorn and vinegar heighten the natural flavors of oysters without overpowering the pleasant brininess of the oyster.

Seafood
Barbecue Sauce

MAKES 2 CUPS

2½ cups honey

1 cup rice vinegar

½ cup soy sauce

1 cup ketchup

2 cinnamon sticks

1 tablespoon Sriracha chili sauce

1 tablespoon whole coriander seeds

1 tablespoon fresh ginger, peeled and chopped

1 tablespoon whole black peppercorns

½ cup fresh cilantro, chopped

¼ cup fresh lime juice

In a medium sauce pan, combine all ingredients together and bring to a simmer over medium heat. Allow to cook for 20-30 minutes until sauce is reduced by about half. Strain through a fine strainer and allow to thicken as it cools before using.

Smoked Red Chili
Chimichurri

MAKES 2½ CUPS

2-3 chipotle peppers (canned en adobo)

1 tablespoon garlic, chopped

3 bay leaves

1 bunch cilantro, stems removed

1 lime, zested

1 bunch Italian parsley, stems removed

½ cup green onions, chopped

1 cup white vinegar

½ cup extra virgin olive oil

1 tablespoon honey

1 teaspoon ground cumin

1 tablespoon dried oregano

Kosher salt

Black pepper

Place all ingredients into a food processor and pulse until smooth. Season with salt and pepper.

This recipe goes with the Wagyu Flat Iron Steak, page 128. It can also be used to marinate chicken wings before grilling.

Oysters with Red Wine Mignonette Sauce page 42

Smooth Mustard Sauce for Seafood

3 tablespoons dry mustard

1 cup mayonnaise

1 tablespoon Worcestershire sauce

½ tablespoon A1 Steak Sauce

3 tablespoons heavy cream

¼ teaspoon ground black pepper

½ teaspoon Old Bay seasoning

Pinch cayenne pepper

¾ teaspoon kosher salt

Place all the ingredients into a food processor and puree on high until very smooth. Scrape sides with rubber spatula and continue to blend for 2 more minutes. Place in the refrigerator for one hour to chill before using.

This sauce is perfect for stone crab claws and anything to do with crab.

Southern Comfort and Peach Barbecue Sauce

MAKES 1 QUART

4 teaspoons soy sauce

4 teaspoons Worcestershire sauce

½ teaspoon ground allspice

5 teaspoons Blackened Spice, page 178

1¾ cups barbecue sauce

⅔ cup lemon juice

1 teaspoon liquid smoke

¾ cup brown sugar

¾ cup ketchup

½ cup fresh peaches, peeled and chopped fine

½ cup Southern Comfort

Combine all ingredients except the Southern Comfort in a heavy bottom sauce pan. Bring sauce to a slow boil. Reduce heat to low and simmer for 30-45 minutes. Remove from heat and whisk in the Southern Comfort. Allow sauce to cool slightly and transfer to a storage container. Store sauce in the refrigerator for up to 2 weeks.

This sauce goes with the Bourbon Marinated Pork Chops, page 114.

Spicy Asian Style Mustard Sauce

MAKES 2 CUPS

½ cup sugar

¼ cup dry mustard

2 egg yolks

½ cup red wine vinegar

¾ teaspoon kosher salt

1½ teaspoons crushed red pepper

¾ cup sour cream

1 tablespoon green onion, minced

In a small metal mixing bowl, combine the sugar, dry mustard, egg yolks, red wine vinegar, salt and crushed red pepper. Place over a small sauce pan of simmering water. Stirring mixture every few minutes, cook until a thin pudding-like consistency is achieved. Remove bowl from heat and allow to cool to room temperature. When cool, fold in the sour cream and the minced green onions and mix well. Keep refrigerated until needed.

Chefs have many reasons for creating sauces with the top 3 being; cooking medium, tenderizer and flavor enhancement. The main one we concentrate on in this book is flavor enhancer. Try to make your sauces as a compliment to your food and not overpowering. Many a time a young chef will inadvertently overpower a dish with a robust sauce. You should be able to pick out the flavors of the food you are saucing as well and the flavors in the sauce. Doing this requires that the sauce be balanced between, sweet, salty, spicy and sour. Sauce making is truly an art form and can take a long time to master, but that doesn't mean you shouldn't try.

SAUCES · THE BASICS · 44

Bourbon Marinated Pork Chop with Southern Comfort Peach Barbecue Sauce page 44

Sriracha Chili Ketchup

MAKES 1 CUP

½ cup ketchup

½ cup Sriracha chili sauce

2 teaspoons fish sauce

2 tablespoons sugar

2 limes, juiced

Whisk all ingredients together until smooth. Use to dip chicken or pork steaks or even glaze your meatloaf recipe. Store leftovers in the refrigerator for up to 1 week.

This ketchup is great for dipping any fried seafood and, of course, french fries!

Steak Diane Sauce

MAKES 2 CUPS

1 cup Basic Veal Sauce, page 50

½ cup heavy cream

2 tablespoons Grey Poupon mustard

2 tablespoons Worcestershire sauce

¾ teaspoon fresh thyme leaves, chopped

Kosher salt

Black pepper

In a sauce pan, add all of the ingredients and bring to a boil. Reduce heat to a simmer, whisking often, for 20 minutes. Remove from heat and season with salt and pepper. Keep warm until needed.

This recipe goes with the Steak Diane recipe, page 126.

Sweet and Spicy Chili Dipping Sauce

MAKES 2 CUPS

½ cup Mae Ploy Sweet Chili Sauce

½ cup mayonnaise

1 cup Spicy Asian Style Mustard Sauce, page 44

1 teaspoon fresh cilantro, minced

Whisk all ingredients together until smooth. Keep refrigerated until needed.

This sauce goes with the Sweet and Spicy Rock Shrimp recipe on page 74.

Sriracha chili sauce is a Thai hot sauce made from red Thai chilies, vinegar, sugar, garlic and salt. It can be found in almost every major grocery chain.

Veal Chop Dijonnaise (Made from Diane Sauce) page 46

Sweet Potato Gravy with Grand Marnier

MAKES 3 CUPS

2 tablespoons duck fat or butter

¾ cup white onions, chopped

1½ cups sweet potatoes, peeled and finely chopped

½ teaspoon garlic, minced

1 bay leaf

1 teaspoon kosher salt

¼ teaspoon white pepper

¼ teaspoon cayenne pepper

½ teaspoon dry mustard

½ teaspoon dried thyme leaves

6 cups Chicken Stock, page 52

5 tablespoons brown sugar

1 cup sweet potatoes, peeled and ½" diced

2 tablespoons Grand Marnier

⅓ cup green onions, chopped

In a medium sauce pan, sauté the onions in the fat until they start to brown, about 8-10 minutes, stirring occasionally. Add the first addition of sweet potatoes (1½ cups), cook for 10 minutes, stirring until potatoes start to brown. Add the garlic, bay leaf and half of the seasonings. Stir in 2 cups of stock and boil for 8-10 minutes. Add half of the sugar and cook for 4 more minutes. Add another 2 cups of stock and the remaining sugar and allow to simmer for another 15 minutes. Puree mixture and strain into a clean sauce pan. Add the rest of the stock, the other half of the seasonings and the remaining ingredients (including 1 cup sweet potatoes). Bring sauce to a simmer and allow to reduce to about 3 cups, stirring occasionally.

The Best Bleu Cheese Sauce

MAKES 3 CUPS

4 tablespoons whole butter

4 tablespoons flour

2 cups Half & Half

⅛ teaspoon white pepper

⅛ teaspoon cayenne pepper

Pinch nutmeg

Kosher salt

1 cup bleu cheese crumbles

1 tablespoon chives, chopped

In a small sauce pan, over medium heat, melt the butter and slowly whisk in the flour until smooth. Reduce heat to low and cook, stirring continually, for 3-4 minutes. Slowly whisk in the Half & Half, white pepper, cayenne pepper, nutmeg and season with salt. Bring sauce to a simmer, stirring often, and cook for 5-6 minutes. Turn off heat and fold in the bleu cheese crumbles and chopped chives. Keep warm until needed. Refrigerate any leftovers for up to 7 days.

This sauce was created to go with the Bleu Cheese Potato Chips on page 64, but is also wonderful with blackened scallops, chicken or beef tips.

Traditional Béarnaise Sauce

MAKES 1½ CUPS

1½ cups Hollandaise Sauce, page 38

4 teaspoons Béarnaise Reduction

Whisk ingredients together until smooth and use immediately.

This sauce is great not only on steaks, but over grilled chicken with some crabmeat. Or even lamb chops.

Béarnaise Reduction

1 cup dried tarragon leaves

⅓ cup white wine

1½ cups red wine vinegar

¼ teaspoon garlic, minced

2 teaspoons shallots, minced

½ teaspoon dried thyme leaves

In a small sauce pan, combine all the ingredients and cook over low heat until mixture is almost dry; about 90% of the liquid has evaporated and mixture is a thick paste. Store in the refrigerator until needed.

Filet and Blackened Scallops with Bleu Cheese Sauce page 48

Truffled
Madeira Sauce

MAKES 1½ CUPS

1   small shallot, minced

1   teaspoon olive oil

½   ounce black truffle peelings, drained and rough chopped

4   teaspoons brandy

¼   cup Madeira

1   cup Basic Veal Sauce, page 50

1½   teaspoons truffle oil

1½   teaspoons flour

Kosher salt

Black pepper

In a small sauce pan, sauté the shallots in the olive oil until soft, about 2-3 minutes. Add the truffle peelings, brandy and Madeira and bring to a boil. Reduce heat slightly and continue to cook until liquid is reduced by half. Add the veal sauce and bring to a simmer. In a small mixing bowl mix the truffle oil and the flour to make a smooth paste. Whisk truffle paste into the sauce and continue to cook for 15 more minutes. Season with salt and pepper and keep warm until needed.

Vanilla Bean
Butter Sauce

MAKES 2 CUPS

2   tablespoons shallots, minced

1   cup white wine

1   vanilla bean, split and scraped

1   cup heavy cream

1   teaspoon brown sugar

2   sticks cold, unsalted butter, cut into cubes

1-2   drops vanilla extract

Kosher salt

White pepper

In a small sauce pan, combine the shallots and white wine and bring to a boil, cooking until almost dry with about 2 tablespoons remaining. Add the vanilla bean, heavy cream and the brown sugar and reduce mixture by half. Turn heat off and whisk in the butter, 1 tablespoon at a time, waiting until it is fully incorporated before adding the next tablespoon. When all the butter is incorporated remove the vanilla bean and whisk in the vanilla extract and season with salt and pepper. Serve immediately.

Veal Mother Sauce
(Basic Veal Sauce)

MAKES 1 QUART

⅔   cup Clarified Butter, page 172

1   cup flour

3   tablespoons tomato paste

1   bay leaf

5   cups Beef Stock, page 52

1¾   cups heavy whipping cream

4   tablespoons Madeira

2-3   fresh thyme sprigs

8   ounces veal demi glace

Kosher salt

White pepper

Combine butter and flour in a large sauce pan and cook over low heat, stirring frequently until a light brown, about 5-6 minutes. Add the tomato paste, bay leaf, beef stock, cream, wine and thyme. Whisk until smooth and bring sauce to a slow simmer, stirring and skimming often. Add the veal glace and season liberally with kosher salt and pepper. Continue to simmer for about 45 minutes. Strain through a fine strainer. Store in the refrigerator until needed.

Tournedos Rossini with Truffled Madeira Sauce page 50

Beef Stock

MAKES 1 GALLON

7 pounds beef bones and beef scraps

3 cups yellow onion, chopped

2 cups carrot, chopped

2 cups celery, chopped

1 8-ounce can tomato paste

2 cups dry red wine

2 bay leaves

3-4 fresh thyme sprigs

5-6 fresh parsley stems

8 quarts water

Kosher salt

Black pepper

Place the beef bones and beef scraps in a roasting pan and roast at 400 degrees for 30 minutes. Remove roasting pan from oven and carefully stir in the onions, carrots, celery and tomato paste. Return pan to the oven and continue to roast for another 20-25 minutes. Once again remove the roasting pan from the oven and drain off excess fat. Place the roasting pan on the stove top and deglaze pan with the red wine. Scrape the bottom of the pan for browned particles. Place vegetable mixture into a stock pot; add the herbs, water and a pinch of salt and pepper. Slowly bring liquid to a boil and reduce heat to a simmer. Simmer stock for 5-6 hours, skimming regularly. Remove from heat and strain through a fine strainer.

Chicken Stock

MAKES 5 QUARTS

4 pounds chicken parts and pieces

1 large onion, peeled and quartered

2 cups carrot, chopped

2 cups celery, chopped

1 leek, white part only, cut in half lengthwise and chopped

8 fresh thyme sprigs

8 fresh parsley stems

1 fresh rosemary sprig

2 bay leaves

10 whole peppercorns

2 whole cloves garlic, peeled

2 gallons cold water

Place chicken, vegetables, herbs and spices into a medium stock pot and pour in water. Cook on high heat until it starts to boil. Turn heat down to medium low so that stock maintains a low, gentle simmer. Skim any foam or fat from the stock with a spoon every half hour. Add hot water as needed to keep bones and vegetables submerged. Simmer uncovered for 6-8 hours. Strain stock through a fine mesh strainer into another stock pot and reduce liquid to 5 quarts. Place in refrigerator overnight. Remove solidified fat from surface of liquid and store in container with lid in refrigerator for 2-3 days or in freezer for up to 3 months.

Use as a base for soups and sauces.

Lobster Stock

MAKES 2 QUARTS

2 tablespoons unsalted butter

1 cup yellow onions, chopped

1 cup celery, chopped

1 cup tomatoes, chopped

1 lemon, split in half

2-3 fresh thyme sprigs

1 fresh rosemary sprig

5-6 fresh parsley stems

2 bay leaves

1 teaspoon whole black peppercorns

1 pound lobster and shrimp shells

1 tablespoon tomato paste

¼ cup sherry wine

2 quarts water

Kosher salt

White pepper

In a large stock pot, melt the butter and sweat the onions, celery and tomatoes over medium low heat for 20 minutes, stirring often. Add the rest of the ingredients and bring to a boil. Skim off any foam that rises to the top, reduce heat to low and simmer for 2 hours. Skim stock every 20-30 minutes during the cooking process. Remove stock from heat, lightly season with salt and pepper and allow to cool slightly before straining through a fine mesh strainer or cheese cloth. Keep warm until needed.

Braised Pork Osso Bucco page 52

Mediterranean Vegetable Broth

MAKES 1 QUART

1 tablespoon olive oil

¼ cup red onion, minced

¼ cup fresh fennel, chopped

¼ cup carrots, chopped

1 tablespoon garlic, minced

1 cup tomatoes, diced

1 cup white wine

½ cup vodka

1½ cups tomato juice

2 tablespoons basil pesto

Pinch crushed red pepper

1 teaspoon sugar

Kosher salt

Black pepper

In a medium sauce pan, over medium heat, sauté the red onions, fennel, carrots and the garlic in the olive oil until soft, stirring often, about 5-6 minutes. Add the tomatoes and continue to cook for another 3-4 minutes. Add the rest of the ingredients, season with salt and pepper and bring to a boil. Reduce heat to a simmer and cook for 10 more minutes. Store leftovers in the refrigerator for up to 4 days.

This sauce can be used for all varieties of seafood like shrimp, scallops and salmon. It is perfect for cooking mussels.

Bourbon and Brown Sugar Brine

MAKES 1 QUART

½ cup Knob Creek (or any other high quality bourbon)

1 bay leaf

1 tablespoon garlic, minced

4 sprigs fresh rosemary

2 sprigs fresh thyme

⅔ cup brown sugar

2 tablespoons kosher salt

1½ teaspoons black pepper

3½ cups ice water

In a small sauce pan, combine the bourbon with the bay leaf, garlic, rosemary and thyme sprigs, brown sugar, kosher salt and black pepper. Place pan over medium heat and gently heat to a simmer, allowing spices to dissolve. Be very careful not to let it get too hot or catch fire. Mix the bourbon spice mixture with the ice water. Place the brine in the refrigerator until fully chilled. Once cold use it to marinate large cuts of meat such as pork racks, ribs or roasts.

Savory Beer Marinade

MAKES 2½ CUPS

1 12-ounce bottle full bodied beer

3 tablespoons apple cider vinegar

1 tablespoon dry mustard

1½ tablespoons Worcestershire sauce

1½ tablespoons A1 Steak Sauce

6 tablespoons low sodium soy sauce

2 teaspoons garlic, minced

2 teaspoons chipotle powder

2 teaspoons kosher salt

1 teaspoon black pepper

1 teaspoon green onion, minced

1 teaspoon cilantro leaves, minced

Whisk together all ingredients until smooth.

Use to marinate hanger steaks, skirt steak or flat iron steaks before grilling.

Cajun Seasoned Ribeye Marinade

MAKES 1 CUP

⅔ cup Blackened Spice, page 178

4 teaspoons Worcestershire sauce

½ teaspoon liquid smoke

⅔ cup vegetable oil

3-4 drops Tabasco sauce

Whisk all ingredients together in a small mixing bowl until smooth. Rub a tablespoon of marinade on each side of the steak and allow it to sit, covered, in the refrigerator overnight before grilling. Keep any leftovers covered tightly and stored at room temperature.

Steamed Mediterranean Halibut page 54

Garlic and Herb Chicken Brine

MAKES 2 QUARTS

2 cups water

1 cup sugar

2 tablespoons kosher salt

1½ tablespoons garlic, minced

2 fresh rosemary sprigs

3 fresh thyme sprigs

1 rind of a lemon

1 bay leaf

6 cups ice water

In a small sauce pan, combine the first water (2 cups), sugar, kosher salt, chopped garlic, rosemary and thyme sprigs, bay leaf and lemon peel and bring to a boil. Remove mixture from heat and stir in the ice water.

Use to brine chicken for 12-36 hours before grilling. Do not place chicken in the brine container. Pour out the amount of brine you need to submerge the chicken pieces, reserving the balance for another batch. Always discard used brine. Keep unused brine in the refrigerator at all times.

Grilled Herb Chicken Marinade

MAKES 2 CUPS

1¼ cups olive oil

⅔ cup fresh lemon juice

¼ teaspoon cayenne pepper

4 teaspoons paprika

2½ tablespoons dried oregano leaves

1 teaspoon kosher salt

½ teaspoon black pepper

3 bay leaves

½ teaspoon garlic salt

1 teaspoon fresh rosemary, minced

Combine all ingredients in a sauce pan and bring to a boil over medium heat. Reduce heat to a simmer and cook for five minutes. Chill thoroughly before marinating chicken pieces prior to grilling or roasting.

Kentucky Bourbon Marinade

MAKES 4 CUPS

½ cup olive oil

6 tablespoons Dijon mustard

¾ cup Knob Creek (or other high quality bourbon)

¾ cup soy sauce

6 tablespoons red wine vinegar

3 tablespoons Worcestershire sauce

¾ cup brown sugar

3 tablespoons A1 Sauce

6 tablespoons red onion, minced

3 tablespoons garlic, minced

3 tablespoons kosher salt

4 teaspoons black pepper

Whisk all ingredients together until smooth. Store refrigerated until needed. Make sure to stir well before using.

This recipe is used with the Bourbon Marinated Ribeye Steak recipe, page 114, but can also be used with salmon or chicken.

Kentucky Bourbon Marinated Ribeye page 56

Ahi Tuna Wontons with Tartare Sauce page 60

appetizers

Chorizo Duck and Goat Cheese Tart

Pan Fried Crab Cakes with Bourbon Jalapeno Creamed Corn

Eddie's Famous Smoking Shrimp Cocktail

Ahi Tuna Wontons with Tartare Sauce

SERVES 6-8

8 wonton wrappers

1 egg, beaten

1¼ pound fresh ahi tuna loin, trimmed

½ batch Ahi Tuna Wonton Tartare Sauce

1 teaspoon white sesame seeds

1 teaspoon cilantro, chopped

½ cup Creamy Wasabi Sauce, page 32

Preheat oven to 400 degrees. Cut each wonton wrapper into 2 triangles and place on a nonstick cookie sheet. Brush the wonton triangles with the beaten egg and bake until golden brown and crispy, about 10 minutes. While the wontons are baking, trim and finely mince the tuna and place into a glass mixing bowl. Add the tuna tartare sauce and toss to fully coat. Place the wonton triangles on a serving platter. Top each wonton with the ahi tuna mixture, sprinkle with sesame seeds and the chopped cilantro and serve with the Creamy Wasabi Sauce on the side.

Ahi Tuna Wonton Tartare Sauce

MAKES 1½ CUPS

2 tablespoons fresh lime juice

½ cup soy sauce

¾ cup Mae Ploy Sweet Chili Sauce

2 teaspoons Sriracha chili sauce

2 tablespoons sweet soy sauce

1½ teaspoons wasabi, powdered

2 teaspoons pickled ginger, minced

1½ teaspoons fresh cilantro, minced

¾ teaspoon fresh mint, minced

1 teaspoon green onions, minced

Place all ingredients into a food processor and pulse until well combined. Refrigerate until needed.

Even though this recipe has a lot of specialty ingredients, most of which can be found at the large grocery store chains, it is well worth the effort to make this sauce. Not only is it perfect with tuna, but you can also use it as a glaze for grilled beef ribs or grilled chicken thighs.

Bacon Wrapped Barbecued Shrimp

MAKES 12 SHRIMP

12 large headless shrimp, 12/14 count or larger

12 bacon slices

4 tablespoons fresh horseradish, grated

6 metal skewers

Kosher salt

Black pepper

¾ cup Southern Comfort Peach Barbecue Sauce, page 44

Lemon Wedges

Preheat oven to 375 degrees and preheat grill to high. Lay pieces of bacon on a baking tray and bake for 4 minutes. Bacon should just start to render the fat. Remove bacon from oven and drain well. Peel and de-vein shrimp and, using a paring knife, split the shrimp halfway through, opening the back of the shrimp all the way from head to tail. Lay one teaspoon of horseradish down the entire back of each shrimp. Wrap one piece of blanched bacon around each shrimp, starting at the head and continuing to the tail with minimal overlap. Lay four pieces of shrimp on a cutting board so that all the tails are on one side and the heads on the other. Place a long skewer through the heads and one long skewer through the tail ends to hold in place while cooking. Continue this to make three sets of shrimp skewers. Season shrimp with salt and pepper and place on the grill for 4-5 minutes until bacon starts to get crispy. Flip shrimp and brush with the barbeque sauce. Continue to cook for another 4 minutes. Flip again and continue to baste with the barbecue sauce until shrimp is cooked and bacon is crispy. Serve with lemon wedges.

Bacon Wrapped Barbecued Shrimp page 60

Baked Brie En Croute with Cherry Jam

SERVES 3-4

1 sheet puff pastry dough, defrosted

1 8-ounce Brie cheese wheel

2 tablespoons Cherry Jam, page 6

¼ cup Candied Pecans, page 96

1 lightly beaten egg

Crackers

Fresh green apple slices

Raspberries

Fresh mint leaves

Preheat oven to 375 degrees. Lay the puff pastry out on a flat surface. Place the Brie in the center of the pastry and top Brie with the Cherry Jam and Candied Pecans. Gather up the edges of the pastry, pressing around the Brie, and gather at the top. Gently squeeze the excess dough and tie together with a piece of kitchen string. Place Brie on a cookie sheet and brush the pastry surface with the beaten egg. Bake Brie in the oven for 20 minutes until pastry is golden brown. Remove kitchen string and serve with the crackers, apple slices, raspberries and mint leaves.

Beef Carpaccio with Arugula Salad

SERVES 3-4

8-10 ounces beef tenderloin tips

Sea salt

Black pepper

3 tablespoons extra virgin olive oil

2 tablespoons aged balsamic vinegar

2 tablespoons capers

2 tablespoons red onion, minced

4 cups arugula

2-3 ounce Parmesan cheese block

Wrap the tender loin tips tightly in plastic wrap and place in the freezer for 2 hours. After 2 hours, unwrap the beef and slice into approximately 1/8 inch slices. Lay the slices out on plastic wrap that has been lightly oiled with the olive oil. Top with another piece of plastic and gently pound with a meat mallet until the beef is paper thin. Repeat process until all the meat is sliced and pounded. Place the meat on a chilled, large serving platter. Sprinkle meat with salt and pepper. Drizzle half the olive oil and vinegar onto the beef. Sprinkle half the capers and onions on the beef. Combine the remaining oil and vinegar with the remaining capers and onion and toss with the arugula. Mound the salad mixture on top of the Carpaccio. Using a vegetable peeler, shave the Parmesan cheese over the salad.

This recipe is great served with the Rosemary Cheese Polenta, page 164.

Black and Bleu Beef Bruschetta

MAKES 12 PIECES

1 loaf French bread

Extra virgin olive oil

Sea salt

½ pound prime beef tips, trimmed and julienned

¼ cup onions, julienned

1 teaspoon Blackened Spice, page 178

½ Bacon and Gorgonzola Cheese Crust, page 26

3 cherry tomatoes, cut into fourths

1 teaspoon chives, chopped

Slice the bread on the bias into 2 inch long slices about ½ inch thick, until you have 12 pieces. Place bread slices on a cookie sheet, brush each slice with olive oil and sprinkle with sea salt. Bake in the oven for 4-5 minutes until lightly toasted. While toasting, heat 1 tablespoon of olive oil in a small skillet until hot. Toss the beef tips with the Blackened Spice and sear in the hot oil until golden brown on all sides. Add the onions to the pan and continue to cook for 3-4 minutes until onions are soft and beef is cooked. Remove from heat and evenly divide the beef/onion mixture on top of the toast points. Scoop 2 teaspoons of the Bacon Cheese Crust on top of each bruschetta and place in the oven for 5-6 minutes until cheese starts to brown. Remove and transfer to a serving platter. Top each bruschetta with a cherry tomato fourth and some of the chopped chives.

Baked Brie En Croute with Cherry Jam page 62

Bleu Cheese Potato Chips

SERVES 4-6

2 pounds large baking potatoes

1½ cups Bleu Cheese Sauce, page 48

Kosher salt

Black pepper

3 ounces bleu cheese, crumbled

½ cup bacon, chopped, crisply cooked

2 teaspoons fresh parsley, chopped

Preheat fryer to 350 degrees. Using a mandolin or slicer, slice potatoes paper-thin and place into a bowl filled with ice water. Allow potatoes to soak for about 20 minutes, drain and re-fill with clean water. Gently swish potatoes around in the water and drain for a second time. Allow to drain for about 20 minutes. Gently heat the Bleu Cheese Sauce until hot and keep warm. In batches, deep fry the potato slices until crispy, drain briefly, season with salt and pepper and place into a large serving bowl. Pour the warm Bleu Cheese Sauce over the potato chips and sprinkle with the bleu cheese crumbles, chopped bacon and parsley.

Buttermilk Fried Lobster

SERVES 3-4

2 5-6 ounce lobster tails

Kosher salt

Black pepper

½ cup flour

½ cup buttermilk

¼ cup Five Cheese Sauce, page 36

1½ ounces Lobster Butter, page 174

2 cups Bleu Cheese Cole Slaw, page 156

2 teaspoons fresh chives, chopped

Lemon Wedges

Preheat fryer to 350 degrees. Split the lobster tails in half, lengthwise, and remove from their shells. Liberally season the 4 pieces of lobster with kosher salt and black pepper. Dredge each piece in the flour, then in the buttermilk and again in the flour. Deep fry breaded lobster tails for about 4 minutes until just barely cooked through. Drain briefly and season again with salt and pepper. While the lobsters are frying, gently heat the Five Cheese Sauce in a small sauté pan with the Lobster Butter and whisk until smooth. Remove from heat and keep warm. Spoon the coleslaw onto the bottom of a serving platter, shingle the finished lobster tail pieces on top of the slaw and spoon the butter/cheese sauce around the slaw/lobster. Sprinkle with chopped chives and serve with lemon wedges.

Chef Matt's Meatballs

MAKES 12 LARGE

¼ cup red onions, minced

1 tablespoon garlic, minced

¼ cup extra virgin olive oil

1½ teaspoons ground black pepper

½ teaspoon crushed red pepper

1½ teaspoons dried basil leaf

Kosher salt

⅓ cup Parmesan cheese, grated

1 large egg, beaten

¼ cup frozen chopped spinach, thawed

⅓ cup Panko bread crumbs

¼ pound ground lamb

½ pound ground pork

½ pound ground prime chuck

12 cubes (about 5 ounces) fresh mozzarella cheese, cut into ½ inch cubes

3 cups Basic Tomato-Basil Sauce, page 28

¼ cup red wine

1 tablespoon extra virgin olive oil

1 tablespoon fresh basil, chopped

Preheat oven to 375 degrees. In a small sauté pan, over medium heat, sweat the onions and garlic until soft. Add the black pepper, crushed red pepper, dried basil and a generous amount of salt. Continue to cook for 3-4 minutes. Transfer herb mixture to the refrigerator until cold. When mixture is well chilled, place into a mixing bowl and add the Parmesan cheese, egg, spinach, bread crumbs, lamb, pork and beef.

Chef Matt's Meatballs-continued

Mix until fully incorporated. Divide mixture into 12 equal balls, about 2.5 ounces each. Flatten each ball into a hamburger patty shape and place one piece of mozzarella cheese in the center of each patty. Fold the patty around the cheese and pinch closed all the seams to make sure the cheese is fully encased in the meat mixture.

Place the meatballs in a casserole dish and bake in the oven for 20 minutes. Remove from oven and carefully drain any grease. Add the tomato sauce and the red wine to the casserole dish, toss gently and cover with foil. Place back in the oven for 15 more minutes until hot. Remove from oven and remove foil. Drizzle the meatballs with the extra virgin olive oil and sprinkle with chopped basil.

Buttermilk Fried Lobster page 64

Crab Cocktail with Mustard Sauce

SERVES 3-4

2 cups iceberg lettuce, shredded

½ cup Smooth Mustard Sauce, page 44

1 pound jumbo lump crab meat

1 teaspoon fresh chives, minced

Cracked black pepper

Lemon wedges

Saltine crackers

Place the iceberg lettuce in the bottom of a chilled serving bowl. Spoon the mustard sauce on top of the lettuce. Being careful not to break up the crab meat, place it on top of the dressing. Top crab with minced chives, a generous amount of freshly cracked pepper and serve with the lemon wedges and crackers.

This appetizer has been on and off our menu over the years and is officially not on the menu now, but unofficially, we still make it for those who love it and request it every time they come!

Crab Stuffed Portobello Mushrooms

SERVES 4-6

4 large portobello mushrooms

1 batch Pan Fried Crab Cakes, page 72

6 tablespoons Steak Butter, melted, page 176

4 tablespoons white wine

4 tablespoons bread crumbs

2 tablespoons Parmesan cheese, grated

Fresh parsley, chopped

Lemon wedges

Preheat oven to 400 degrees. Trim the stems from the mushrooms and, using a spoon, remove the gills from the underside of the mushrooms. Place the mushrooms in a baking dish. Divide the crab cake mixture and top each mushroom evenly. Gently melt the Steak Butter in the microwave and pour over the mushrooms. Add the white wine to the dish. Top each mushroom evenly with the bread crumbs and Parmesan cheese. Bake in the oven for 20 minutes or until mushrooms are soft and the tops are a golden brown. Sprinkle dish with the chopped parsley and serve with the lemon wedges.

Calamari Batter

MAKES 2 CUPS

½ cup flour

½ cup corn starch

¼ teaspoon baking soda

¼ teaspoon kosher salt

2 teaspoons black sesame seeds

Crispy Fried Sesame Calamari

MAKES 4-6

2 pounds calamari, cut into ½" rings

Flour

1 batch Calamari Batter

Kosher salt

Black pepper

Lemon wedges

Garlic-Ginger Dipping Sauce, page 36

Spicy Asian Style Mustard Sauce, page 44

Creamy Wasabi Sauce, page 32

Rinse and dry calamari rings. Preheat deep fryer to 375 degrees. Dredge calamari rings in flour and shake off excess. Place floured calamari in a small mixing bowl and ladle in a generous amount of Calamari Batter. Toss well. Working in batches, if necessary, carefully drop the calamari into the hot fryer and cook for 2 minutes, being careful not to overcook. Remove from fryer and season generously with salt and pepper. Serve with the lemon wedges and the three sauces on the side.

1 egg, lightly beaten

¾ teaspoon rice vinegar

¾ teaspoon sesame oil

1½ cups plain soda water

Mix all dry ingredients together. Mix all wet ingredients together and pour over the dry and mix lightly. It is okay to have some lumps. Thin with more soda water if batter seems thick. It should be the consistency of a runny pancake batter.

Crispy Fried Sesame Calamari page 66

Cherry Duck and Goat Cheese Tart

SERVES 4

4 4-inch precooked savory tart shells

¾ cup Cherry Jam

1 batch Duck Filling

¾ pound goat cheese, crumbled

2 teaspoons fresh chives, chopped

12 drops 10 year aged balsamic vinegar

Preheat oven to 375 degrees. Place the four tart shells on a cookie sheet and spoon about 2 teaspoons Cherry Jam into the bottom of each shell. Divide the duck filling between the four shells and evenly divide the rest of the Cherry Jam over the duck filling. Top each shell with 3 ounces goat cheese. Place the tarts into the oven for 12-15 minutes until hot and the goat cheese is starting to brown.   Remove tarts from the oven, sprinkle with the chopped chives and a few drips of the aged balsamic vinegar.

Cherry Jam

Makes 1 cup

2 teaspoons shallot, chopped

¾ cup dried cherries

1¼ cups red wine

5 tablespoons balsamic vinegar

¼ cup sugar

1 tablespoon honey

Water - optional

Duck Filling for Goat Cheese Tart

SERVES 4

1 8-ounce duck breast with skin

Kosher salt

Black pepper

2 cups yellow onion, julienned

¾ cup balsamic vinegar

Score an "x" pattern in the duck skin, being careful not to go into the meat. Season duck breast with salt and pepper. Place into a cold sauté pan, fat side down, and cook slowly over medium heat until all the fat is rendered and the skin is golden brown and crispy. Flip the duck breast and allow it to cook over medium heat for about 15 minutes until cooked medium. Remove duck from pan and let cool completely. With the pan still on the heat, add the onions to the hot fat and continue to cook until golden brown. Drain any excess grease from the pan and deglaze pan with the balsamic vinegar. Reduce until almost dry. Remove from heat and allow to cool completely. Shave the cooled duck breast on a mandolin or meat slicer and toss with the balsamic onions

In a small sauce pan combine the shallots, dried cherries, red wine, balsamic vinegar and sugar. Bring to a boil, reduce heat to medium and continue to cook until almost dry. Be careful not to burn. Remove from heat and allow to cool slightly before adding to a food processor. Add the honey and puree on high for 3-4 minutes until very smooth. Add a touch of water if mixture seems a little thick. It will get thicker as it cools. Makes 1 cup.

Eddie's Famous Shrimp Cocktail

MAKES 6-8 SERVINGS

3½ quarts water

2 lemons, halved

1 small onion, peeled and halved

4 tablespoons kosher salt

¾ teaspoon cayenne pepper

1 teaspoon white pepper

3 tablespoons Old Bay seasoning

3 bay leaves

3 tablespoons pickling spice

16-20 count size shell-on shrimp

In a large pot bring the water to a boil; add lemons, onion, salt, cayenne pepper, white pepper and Old Bay seasoning. Put the pickling spice and the bay leaves into a cheese cloth and tightly tie with twine. Add to the stock. Turn stock down to a low boil and allow to cook for 30-45 minutes. Using a pair of tongs, remove the lemons, onions and the spice package. Fill a bowl with ice water. Turn up stock to high and cook shrimp in the boiling liquid in 2 pound batches for 5 minutes. Using a wire skimmer, transfer shrimp to the ice bath and repeat the process, allowing water to return to a boil before adding more shrimp. Drain shrimp and when fully chilled, peel and de-vein. Serve with Eddies's Cocktail Sauce, page 34.

Cherry Duck and Goat Cheese Tart page 68

Florida Stone Crab Claws

SERVES 3-4

1 pound crushed ice

3 pounds stone crab claws, large or jumbo

¾ cup Smooth Mustard Sauce, page 44

Lemon wedges

Place the crushed ice into a large serving bowl. Wrap each stone crab claw in a kitchen towel and hit with a hammer just enough to crack the claws without destroying them. Place the cracked claws in the crushed ice and serve with the mustard sauce on the side with the lemon wedges.

This popular appetizer is a seasonal favorite which ranges from the end of October to the middle of May. We generally serve them during the first part of the New Year when the market price has had time to stabilize.

Grilled Scallop Ceviche

SERVES 6-8

2 pounds large fresh scallops

1 tablespoon extra virgin olive oil

Kosher salt

Black pepper

¾ cup fresh lime, juiced and zested

2 tablespoons extra virgin olive oil

½ teaspoon ground cumin

½ teaspoon ground coriander

½ teaspoon cayenne pepper

2 teaspoons honey

¾ teaspoon kosher salt

¼ cup red onion, diced

¼ cup red pepper, diced

1 tablespoon jalapeño, minced

1 teaspoon fresh cilantro, chopped

Lime wedges

Corn tortilla chips

Preheat grill to high. Rub scallops with the first quantity of olive oil, season with salt and pepper and grill over the hottest part of the grill. Cook only for about 1 minute per side. The scallops should still be rare inside with good char marks on the outside. Set aside to cool. In a small mixing bowl combine the lime juice and zest, olive oil, ground cumin, coriander, cayenne, honey, salt, red onion, red pepper and jalapeño and mix until well combined. Cut the cooled scallops into 1-inch pieces and add to the Ceviche liquid. Place Ceviche in the refrigerator for 3-4 hours before serving. When ready to serve, add chopped cilantro and serve with lime wedges and corn tortilla chips.

Hoisin Barbecue Chicken Wings

MAKES 8-10 SERVINGS

50 chicken wings

2 x batch of Garlic and Herb Chicken Brine, page 54

2 x batch of Hoisin Barbecue Sauce, page 36

2 tablespoons white sesame seeds

2 tablespoons fresh cilantro, chopped

Combine the chicken wings with the Garlic and Herb Chicken Brine in a container with a tight fitting lid and refrigerate overnight. Preheat deep fryer to 350 degrees. Drain chicken wings from the brine and discard used brine. Pat wings dry with paper towels and, working in batches if needed, fry the chicken wings for 7-8 minutes until golden brown and cooked all the way through. Transfer wings to a large mixing bowl and toss with the Hoisin Barbecue Sauce, white sesame seeds and chopped cilantro.

This is a favorite at our off site catering events. Everyone loves sweet, spicy and salty chicken wings. If you don't have a deep fryer, don't be afraid to grill the wings. It's a 50/50 split on which way tastes better.

Florida Stone Crab Claws page 70

SERVES 3-4

Mediterranean Style Mussels

2 pounds fresh, west coast mussels

1 batch Mediterranean Vegetable Broth, page 54

4 tablespoons Steak Butter, page 176

1 lemon

2 teaspoons fresh parsley, chopped

1 loaf French style bread

Wash and de-beard mussels. Discard any that are open. In a sauce pan, with a tight fitting lid bring the Mediterranean Vegetable Broth and the Steak Butter to a boil. Add the mussels and cover. Cook mussels for 3-4 minutes, until mussels are fully open. Discard any mussels that are not open. Pour the mussels and broth into a large serving bowl. Squeeze the lemon over the mussels and sprinkle with the chopped parsley. Serve with the bread to dip in the broth.

West coast mussels are a little harder to find in the Midwest compared to the P.E.I. species that comes from the east coast. The west coast variety is generally larger and sweeter with a velvety texture. They are worth every effort to find.

Pan Fried Crab Cakes

MAKES 4 CAKES

1 large egg, lightly beaten

¼ cup mayonnaise

½ teaspoon Worcestershire sauce

½ teaspoon Dijon mustard

3 tablespoons Clarified Butter, page 172

½ teaspoon kosher salt

½ teaspoon black pepper

2 teaspoons fresh parsley, chopped

¼ teaspoon Old Bay seasoning

4 tablespoons Panko bread crumbs

1 pound lump crab meat

4 tablespoons Clarified Butter

¼ cup A Really Good Tartare Sauce, page 26

1 teaspoon chives, minced

Lemon wedges

In a medium mixing bowl, combine the first 10 ingredients and mix until very smooth. Gently fold in the crab meat, being careful not to break up the crab too much, but also making sure mixture is thoroughly combined. Portion mixture into 4-5 ounce cakes. Refrigerate crab cakes for 1 hour to firm before cooking.

In a medium sauté pan, heat butter over medium heat until hot. Add the crab cakes and fry until golden brown on one side, about 4-5 minutes. Flip crab cakes, lower heat slightly and continue to cook until heated through and golden brown. Remove crab cakes from pan and pat dry on paper towels. Place crab cakes on a serving platter and top each with a little tartare sauce and minced chives. Serve with lemon wedges.

Rum and Honey Black Bean Salsa

MAKES 4 CUPS

1 red pepper, diced

1 jalapeño pepper, minced

1 small red onion, diced

2 tablespoons olive oil

⅔ cup dark rum

4 cups black beans, cooked

⅓ cup honey

4 tablespoons fresh cilantro, chopped

4 tablespoons green onion, chopped

Kosher salt

Black pepper

In a large sauté pan, sauté red pepper, jalapeño and red onion in olive oil until soft, about 2 minutes. Add the rum and reduce by 25%. Remove from heat and pour into a mixing bowl. Allow mixture to cool to room temperature and then fold in the remaining ingredients. Season with salt and pepper.

This recipe goes with the Voodoo Jerked Chicken, but can also be used as a great party appetizer. Just serve with warm tortilla chips. You could also fold in some cooked shrimp or chicken into any leftovers for a quick lunch the next afternoon.

Pan Fried Crab Cakes page 72

Spinach and Artichoke Dip

SERVES 6-8

1 16-ounce box frozen chopped spinach

¼ cup onion, minced

1 tablespoon garlic, minced

1 tablespoon olive oil

4 tablespoons full bodied beer

½ pound cream cheese, softened

2 cups frozen artichoke hearts, thawed

3 tablespoons heavy cream

3 ounces pepper jack cheese, shredded

2 ½ ounces Parmesan cheese, grated

1 tablespoon fresh lemon juice

½ teaspoon crushed red pepper

½ teaspoon Tabasco sauce

4 teaspoons sugar

½ teaspoon kosher salt

¼ teaspoon black pepper

4 ounces Cheddar cheese, shredded

Tortilla chips or toast points

Thaw the spinach, ring out excess water and set aside. Pre-heat oven to 350 degrees. In a small sauté pan, cook the onion and garlic in the olive oil until soft and lightly browned. Deglaze pan with the beer and reduce until dry. Allow mixture to cool to room temperature. In a large mixing bowl, mix the spinach with the cooled onion mixture and all remaining ingredients except the Cheddar cheese. Mix well until thoroughly combined. Place dip into a casserole dish, cover with the shredded Cheddar cheese, cover and bake for 35-40 minutes until hot and bubbly. Serve with tortilla chips or toast points.

Sweet and Spicy Rock Shrimp

SERVES 3-4

1½ pounds fresh Florida rock shrimp

½ cup flour

1 batch Calamari Batter, page 66

½ cup Sweet and Spicy Chili Dipping Sauce, page 46

Sriracha chili sauce

4 cups iceberg lettuce, shredded

Cilantro sprigs

Lemon wedges

Preheat fryer to 375 degrees. Toss the shrimp with the flour and shake off excess. In a small bowl add the floured shrimp and just enough calamari batter to lightly coat the shrimp. Carefully add the rock shrimp to the fryer and cook for 3-4 minutes until golden brown. Drain briefly and transfer to a clean mixing bowl. Toss with the Sweet and Spicy Chili Dipping Sauce until thoroughly coated. While the shrimp are cooking, stripe a serving platter with a generous amount of Sriracha chili sauce. Top with shredded lettuce and place the fried rock shrimp on top of the lettuce. Garnish the shrimp with cilantro sprigs and serve with lemon wedges.

Tempura Green Beans

SERVES 4-6

1 pound fresh green beans, trimmed

½ cup flour

1 batch Calamari Batter, page 66

Kosher salt

Black pepper

Creamy Wasabi Sauce, page 32

Preheat fryer to 350 degrees. Toss the green beans in the flour and shake off excess flour. Dip the beans into the Calamari Batter and deep fry at 350 degrees until crispy, about 3 minutes. Drain and season with salt and pepper. Serve with Creamy Wasabi Sauce on the side.

If you don't have a table top fryer, then this recipe is your excuse to buy one. Even if this recipe is the only thing you use it for, it will still be worth it. These are very addicting and some nights we wonder how many of these beans we can sell before our customers get tired of them. Right now there is no end in sight.

Sweet and Spicy Rock Shrimp page 74

French Onion Soup page 82

soups

Crab and Corn Chowder

Tomato and Fresh Vegetable Gazpacho

Cream of Broccoli and Three Cheese Soup

Campfire Chicken and Lime Soup

MAKES 6-8 SERVINGS

2 fresh ears of corn, shucked

1 red pepper

1 jalapeño pepper

1½ tablespoons olive oil

1 pound chicken breast, ½"diced

2 teaspoons ground cumin

½ teaspoon kosher salt

1 small yellow onion, minced

1½ tablespoons roasted garlic cloves

2 tablespoons tomato paste

6 cups Chicken Stock, page 52

¼ cup corn starch

¼ cup water

3 tablespoons fresh cilantro, chopped

2 tablespoons fresh lime juice

Kosher salt

Black pepper

Lime Wedges

Chilled Fresh Strawberry Soup

MAKES 4 SERVINGS

½ cup sugar

¼ cup water

1½ pints fresh strawberries, stem removed

4 ounces mascarpone cheese

4 tablespoons heavy whipping cream

⅛ teaspoon black pepper

⅛ teaspoon kosher salt

Sour Cream

Fresh mint, chopped

In a small sauce pan, combine the sugar and water and bring to a simmer. Remove from heat and refrigerate until cold. In a food processor combine the rest of the ingredients with the sugar/water mixture and puree until smooth. Refrigerate for at least an hour before serving.

Serve in chilled soup bowls and garnish with a touch of sour cream and some freshly chopped mint.

Crab and Corn Chowder

MAKES 4-6 SERVINGS

5 fresh ears of corn, shucked

1 quart Chicken Stock, page 52

4 sprigs fresh thyme

1 bay leaf

2 ounces bacon, chopped

½ cup onion, chopped

¼ cup carrots, chopped

¼ cup celery, chopped

¼ cup leeks, sliced

1 tablespoon garlic, minced

½ cup bell pepper, chopped

1 teaspoon dried thyme leaves

1 teaspoon dried basil leaves

¼ cup flour

1 cup red potatoes, diced

1 pound lump crabmeat

1 teaspoon kosher salt

1 teaspoon Tabasco sauce

1 cup heavy cream

Fresh chives, minced

Continued on page 80

Campfire Chicken and Lime Soup

CONTINUED

Preheat grill to high. Rub corn, red pepper and jalapeño with a touch of olive oil. Grill until the corn is golden brown and the peppers are charred black on all sides. Set aside and allow to cool.

Cut the corn off the cob and cut the cob itself into 5-6 pieces and reserve. Peel the charred skin off the peppers then seed and dice. Reserve diced peppers and corn kernels.

In a soup pot, heat olive oil over high heat. Add chicken, cumin and kosher salt and brown chicken on all sides. Add onion and roasted garlic and continue to cook for 5 minutes, stirring often. Stir in tomato paste. Add the chicken stock, reserved corn, peppers and corn cob pieces and bring soup to a

boil. Combine corn starch and water to make a smooth paste and whisk into soup. Reduce heat to a simmer and cook for 20 minutes. Remove corn cob pieces. Add chopped cilantro and lime juice and turn off heat. Season with salt and pepper and serve with lime wedges on the side.

Crab and Corn Chowder page 78

Crab and
Corn Chowder

CONTINUED

Using a knife, remove corn kernels from the cobs. Set corn kernels aside. Cut cobs into 2" pieces and combine with the Chicken Stock, thyme sprigs and bay leaf and bring to a simmer over medium low heat for 25 minutes. Strain out corn cobs and herbs and set aside the stock.

While making the corn stock, heat a medium soup pot over medium heat and cook the bacon until crispy, about 5 minutes. Remove bacon and drain on paper towels. Add onions, carrots, celery and leeks to the bacon grease and cook, stirring often, until vegetables are soft, about 5 minutes. Add the garlic, bell peppers, dried thyme and dried basil and cook until fragrant, about 2-3 minutes, stirring often.

Sprinkle the flour into the pot and cook, stirring constantly, for 5 minutes. Add the reserved corn stock to the soup pot and whisk until smooth. Add the potatoes and corn kernels to the pot and bring to a boil, then reduce to a simmer and continue to cook for 20 minutes until potatoes are soft. Season the chowder with salt and Tabasco sauce and stir in the crab meat and cream. Garnish soup with the bacon pieces and minced chives.

Cream of Broccoli
with Three Cheeses

MAKES 6-8 SERVINGS

5 tablespoons unsalted butter

1 small yellow onion, minced

2 teaspoons garlic, minced

½ cup flour

5½ cups Chicken Stock, page 52

¾ pound broccoli florets

⅔ cup heavy cream

3-4 chicken bouillon cubes

1½ ounces mascarpone cheese

2 ounces Gruyere cheese, grated

4 ounces Cheddar cheese, grated

1½ ounces fresh spinach leaves

½ teaspoon white pepper

½ teaspoon dry mustard

Pinch ground nutmeg

1 teaspoon fresh lemon juice

1 teaspoon sugar

Kosher salt

In a soup pot, sweat the onions and garlic in the butter over medium heat until soft, about 5-6 minutes. Whisk in flour to form a paste and cook over medium heat for 4-5 minutes, stirring often. Slowly whisk in the Chicken Stock and bring to a boil. Reduce heat to a simmer. Add the broccoli and cook for 15 minutes. Add the rest of the ingredients. Turn off heat, cover and allow the cheeses to melt, about 10 minutes. Season with salt and puree soup in a food processor until smooth and creamy.

Cream of Mushroom
with Sherry Wine

MAKES 4 SERVINGS

5 tablespoons unsalted butter

5 tablespoons flour

2 tablespoons bacon grease

½ cup yellow onion, minced

½ cup celery, minced

¾ pound button mushrooms, sliced

1 teaspoon dried thyme leaves

½ teaspoon Herbs De Provence

1 bay leaf

⅓ cup sherry wine

2½ cups Chicken Stock, page 52

1 cup heavy cream

1 cup Half & Half

½ teaspoon white pepper

Pinch cayenne pepper

Kosher salt

In a small sauce pan, melt the butter over medium heat and whisk in the flour until smooth. Continue to cook roux, stirring frequently, for another 4-5 minutes. Set roux off to the side. In a large soup pot over medium heat, sauté the onions and celery in the bacon grease until soft, about 4-5 minutes. Add the mushrooms, dried thyme, Herbs de Provence and bay leaf and continue to cook until mushrooms are soft. Raise the heat to high and carefully add the sherry wine and continue to cook for 3-4 more minutes. Add the rest of the ingredients and bring soup to a boil. Reduce heat to a simmer and whisk in the reserved roux until smooth. Allow soup to simmer for 20 minutes. Season with kosher salt and serve.

Cream of Broccoli with Three Cheeses page 80

French Onion Soup

MAKES 4-6 SERVINGS

- 3 tablespoons vegetable oil
- 4 large white onions, 1" diced
- 4 large red onions, 1" diced
- ½ teaspoon kosher salt
- 1 tablespoon sugar
- 1 tablespoon brown sugar
- ¼ cup brandy
- ½ tablespoon Herbs de Provence
- ¾ teaspoon dried thyme leaves
- 2 bay leaves
- 1½ tablespoons garlic, minced
- 6 cups Beef Stock, page 52
- 1 leek, sliced with no heavy green parts
- 4 green onions, chopped
- 2 tablespoons roasted garlic cloves
- 6 beef bouillon cubes
- 3 tablespoons sherry wine
- 2 tablespoons Madeira
- ¼ teaspoon white pepper
- 1 loaf French style bread
- 2 cups Gruyere cheese, grated

French Onion Soup

CONTINUED

In a heavy bottomed soup pot, heat the vegetable oil; add the white and red onions and salt. Stir to coat, reduce heat to low, cover pot and cook for 30-45 minutes, or until onions are a deep mahogany brown. Add the sugar and scrape all brown bits off the bottom of the pot. Continue stirring and scraping for 3-4 more minutes. Turn heat to high and carefully deglaze pot with the brandy and allow to reduce for 2 minutes. Add the rest of the ingredients and bring soup to a slow simmer for 45-60 minutes. Skim any oil off the surface and season with salt.

Slice French bread into ¾ inch slices and butter both sides. Toast slices on griddle until golden brown. Ladle soup into ovenproof bowls, add toasted bread and cover with shredded Gruyere cheese. Place ovenproof bowls on a baking sheet lined with foil. Bake at 350 degrees for 5 minutes or under a hot broiler until golden brown and bubbly.

Lobster Bisque

MAKES 6-8 SERVINGS

- 4 1-pound lobsters
- 2 tablespoons butter
- 4 bay leaves
- 8 fresh thyme sprigs
- 1 tablespoon black peppercorns
- 3 tablespoons tomato paste
- ¼ cup brandy
- Kosher salt
- Black pepper
- ¼ pound thick cut bacon, ½" dice
- 2 large Yukon gold potatoes, ¼" dice
- 1 small yellow onion, minced
- 2 cups heavy cream
- 1 teaspoon dry mustard
- Pinch cayenne pepper

Lobster Bisque-continued

Cook lobster in boiling, salted water for 4 minutes. Strain and plunge into ice bath to stop the cooking. When cool, remove the lobster meat from shells, reserving the meat and shells. Coarsely chop the lobster meat and set aside. In a stock pot, heat the butter over medium high heat. Add lobster shells, bay leaves, thyme, peppercorns and tomato paste and cook, stirring often, until shells start to brown. Carefully deglaze pot with brandy and cook 2-3 more minutes. Add enough water to barely cover the lobster shells. Simmer stock for 45 minutes, then strain through a fine strainer and discard solids.

Place stock back in the pot and simmer until there are about 6 cups left. Season stock with salt and pepper and set aside. In a large soup pot, sauté the bacon over medium heat until fat is rendered and bacon starts to crisp. Add potatoes and onions and cook, stirring often, over low heat for 10 minutes. Add half the reserved lobster stock, heavy cream, mustard and cayenne and bring to a boil, reduce heat and simmer 10 more minutes. Fold in the reserved lobster meat and season with salt and pepper.

Lobster Bisque page 82

New England Clam Chowder

MAKES 8-10 SERVINGS

6 slices bacon

1 cup onion, minced

1 cup celery, diced

2 cups red potato, diced

1 cup carrots, diced

4 6.5 ounce cans chopped clams with juice

¾ cup unsalted butter

¾ cup flour

1 quart heavy cream

1 teaspoon Worcestershire sauce

1 tablespoon red wine vinegar

Kosher salt

Black pepper

1 loaf French style bread

In a large skillet, fry the bacon until crispy and remove. Drain the juice from the clams and add juice to the skillet with the onion, celery, potatoes and carrots. Add water just to cover, bring to a simmer and cook until potatoes are tender. Remove from heat. In a heavy soup pan melt the butter and whisk in the flour until smooth. Cook roux over medium heat, stirring constantly, for 2-3 minutes. Whisk in the cream and stir until thick and smooth. Stir in the clam juice and vegetable mixture and heat until hot. Season with salt and pepper. Thin soup with a touch of water if needed. Turn off the heat and stir in the Worcestershire sauce, red wine vinegar and reserved clams. Portion in to soup bowls and crumble cooked bacon on top.

Serve with a big loaf of French bread.

Potato and Leek with Fresh Thyme

MAKES 4-6 SERVINGS

3 tablespoons unsalted butter

5 leeks, sliced with dark green removed

1 small onion, sliced

¼ cup celery, diced

1¼ pounds Yukon gold potatoes, diced

2 fresh thyme sprigs

Pinch crushed red pepper

3 cups Chicken Stock, page 52

2 cups heavy cream

1 cup sour cream

Kosher salt

White pepper

Crispy Fried Onions, page 100

Fresh chives, chopped

In a heavy bottomed soup pan, melt the butter over medium heat. Add leeks, onion, celery, potatoes, thyme sprigs and a large pinch of salt. Reduce heat slightly and cook vegetables for 20 minutes, stirring often. Add crushed red pepper and Chicken Stock, increase heat and bring to a simmer. Cook until potatoes are very soft, about 30 minutes. Remove thyme sprigs. Add the heavy cream and puree soup until smooth. Fold in sour cream and season with salt and pepper. Garnish the top of the soup with the fried onions and chopped chives.

Prime Beef and Vegetable Soup

MAKES 8-10 SERVINGS

1 pound beef tips, medium diced

2 tablespoons Clarified Butter, page 172

1 teaspoon garlic, minced

2 cups leek, sliced

1 cup celery, diced

1 cup carrots, diced

2 cups tomato, chopped

2 bay leaves

4-5 fresh thyme sprigs

1-2 fresh rosemary sprigs

¾ cup red wine

2 tablespoons balsamic vinegar

2 cups red potato, chopped

2 tablespoons tomato paste

8 cups Beef Stock, page 52

Kosher salt

Black pepper

Season beef tips with a generous amount of salt and pepper. Heat butter in a large soup pot over medium heat. When hot, sear the beef tips until golden brown on all sides. Drain excess grease from the pan and add the garlic, leeks, celery, carrots and tomatoes and cook until vegetables start to soften, about 7-8 minutes. Add the bay leaves, thyme and rosemary. Deglaze pot with the red wine and the balsamic vinegar and allow to reduce by half. Add the potatoes, tomato paste and the beef stock and bring to a boil. Reduce heat to a simmer and cook for about 45 minutes. Season with salt and pepper and serve.

Potato and Leek with Fresh Thyme page 84

Roasted Garlic and White Bean Soup

MAKED 4-6 SERVINGS

SOUPS

86

- 4 bulbs garlic, whole
- 2 teaspoons olive oil
- 6 ounces pancetta, diced
- 1 tablespoon olive oil
- ½ cup onion, minced
- ½ cup carrots, diced
- ½ cup celery, diced
- ½ cup leeks, white and tender green parts, diced
- 2 cups dried white beans
- 6 cups Chicken Stock, page 52
- 1 bouquet garni (see note box)
- 2 teaspoons fresh tarragon, chopped

Kosher salt

Fresh ground black pepper

Preheat oven to 375 degrees. Cut off the top of each garlic bulb and brush liberally with the two teaspoons olive oil. Place into an oven proof container and cover with foil. Roast in the oven for 45-60 minutes until garlic is very soft and light brown. Allow to cool to room temperature. Squeeze out all the garlic from the bulbs and pick out any skin saving the paste for the soup recipe. Over medium heat cook the pancetta in one tablespoon olive oil until most of the fat is rendered and the pancetta is a golden brown. Add the vegetables and cook until translucent and soft. Add the beans, bouquet garni and enough Chicken Stock to cover the beans. Bring to a boil. Reduce heat and simmer uncovered for about 2½ hours. Add stock as necessary to keep beans covered. Cook until beans are soft but still retain their shape. Stir the roasted garlic and tarragon into the soup. Season liberally with salt and pepper.

Roasted Tomato Soup with Parmesan and Pesto

MAKES 4-6 SERVINGS

- 1 tablespoon extra virgin olive oil
- 1 pound tomatoes, quartered
- 1 small yellow onion, quartered
- 2 teaspoons fresh garlic, minced
- 1 teaspoon fresh rosemary, chopped
- ½ teaspoon kosher salt
- ¼ teaspoon black pepper
- ¼ teaspoon dried basil leaves
- ¼ teaspoon dried oregano leaves
- 2 cups Chicken Stock, page 52
- ⅔ cup heavy cream
- 4 teaspoons tomato paste
- 2 teaspoons sugar
- ¼ cup Parmesan cheese, grated

Basil Pesto

Preheat oven to 350 degrees. Combine olive oil, tomatoes, onion, garlic, rosemary, salt, pepper, basil and oregano in a roasting pan and mix well. Place vegetable mixture in the oven for 45 minutes, stirring 3-4 times during the roasting process. Transfer ingredients to a soup pan and add the Chicken Stock, heavy cream, tomato paste and sugar. Slowly heat soup to a simmer and cook for 20 minutes. Season soup with salt and pepper, fold in the Parmesan cheese and turn off heat. Allow soup to cool a bit before transferring to a food processor and pureeing until smooth. Gently reheat if necessary and garnish with a few drops of basil pesto.

Sweet Potato Bisque with Candied Pecans

MAKES 6-8 SERVINGS

- 3 pounds large sweet potatoes
- 2 tablespoons olive oil
- 1 cup onion, diced
- ¾ cup carrots, diced
- ½ cup leeks, sliced
- 2 teaspoons garlic, minced
- 1 vanilla bean, split
- ½ teaspoon kosher salt
- ½ teaspoon ground black pepper
- ¼ teaspoon dry oregano
- ¼ teaspoon curry powder
- ¼ teaspoon ground cumin
- ¼ teaspoon ground coriander
- ⅛ teaspoon cinnamon
- ¼ cup white wine
- 3-4 cups Chicken Stock, page 52
- 1 bouquet garni (see note box)
- 1 cup heavy cream
- ¼ stick butter
- 1-2 tablespoons honey

Sour cream

Candied Pecans, page 96

Bouquet Garni – a fancy term for a few sprigs of your favorite fresh herbs tied together with a piece of kitchen string.

For the Sweet Potato Bisque, use 2 bay leaves, 2 cloves, 4 sprigs fresh thyme, and 5 parsley stems wrapped in cheesecloth.

Sweet Potato Bisque with Candied Pecans page 86

Sweet Potato Bisque with Candied Pecans

CONTINUED

Preheat oven to 375 degrees. Rub sweet potatoes with a touch of olive oil and bake on a cookie sheet until soft, about 45 minutes, and set aside to cool for 15 minutes.

While potatoes are baking, heat the olive oil in a large soup pan over medium heat. Add the onion, carrot, leeks, garlic, vanilla bean, salt and pepper. Cook 3 minutes to sweat the vegetables. Add the oregano, curry powder, cumin, coriander and cinnamon. Turn heat to low and continue to cook another 7-8 minutes, stirring often to make sure the vegetables do not stick to the bottom of the pot. Add the white wine and cook one more minute.

Peel sweet potatoes and rough chop them. Add the chopped sweet potatoes and enough Chicken Stock to cover all the vegetables in the pan. Add the bouquet garni and simmer soup for 20 minutes until the vegetables are very tender. Remove the bouquet garni. Purée the soup in a food processor until very smooth. Strain through a fine strainer and return soup back to the pan over medium low heat. Add the heavy cream and heat until hot. If the soup is too thick, add additional stock to desired consistency. Add the butter and honey, stirring constantly until fully incorporated. Season with salt and pepper to taste. Serve in individual bowls with a dollop of sour cream and some Candied Pecans as garnish.

Texas Red Star Chili with Jalapeño

MAKES 4—6 SERVINGS

½ cup vegetable oil

4 cups yellow onion, minced

½ cup jalapeños, minced

4 pounds ground chuck

1 tablespoon ground cumin

¾ tablespoon dried oregano leaves

¾ tablespoon Blackened Spice, page 178

¾ tablespoon granulated garlic

¾ tablespoon black pepper

½ cup brown sugar

3 12-ounce cans full bodied beer

2 12-ounce cans spicy chili beans with liquid

2 12-ounce cans ground peeled tomatoes

1 cup Texas Cowboy Coffee (very strong coffee)

1 tablespoon cocoa powder

Kosher salt

In a large soup pan, over medium heat, sweat the onions and jalapeños in the vegetable oil until very soft, about 10 minutes. Add the ground beef, cumin, oregano, Blackened Spice, garlic, black pepper and brown sugar. Continue to cook until the meat is browned. Add 2 cans beer (drink the third while the chili is simmering), chili beans, tomatoes, coffee, cocoa powder and a pinch of salt. Bring chili to a boil. Reduce heat to a slow simmer and continue to cook for 1 hour. Taste and adjust seasoning with kosher salt and/or sugar, if needed.

Tomato and Fresh Vegetable Gazpacho

MAKES 2-4 SERVINGS

1 English cucumber, seeded, not peeled

1 cup heirloom tomatoes

¼ cup red onion, peeled

½ jalapeño, not seeded

1 teaspoon garlic, crushed

1 tablespoon fresh cilantro

1 tablespoon fresh basil

¼ cup extra virgin olive oil

2 tablespoons red wine vinegar

1 cup tomato juice

¾ teaspoon Tabasco sauce

1¼ teaspoons sugar

Kosher salt

Black pepper

Sliced avocado

Cut the cucumber, tomatoes, red onion and jalapeño into 1" chunks. Working in batches, if necessary, place the cut vegetables in a food processor with the garlic, basil and cilantro and pulse until coarsely chopped. Do not over process. Empty ingredients into a mixing bowl and combine with the rest of the ingredients. Season liberally with salt and pepper and chill in the refrigerator for 2 hours before serving.

Serve in chilled soup cups, garnish with a few drops of olive oil, sliced avocado and a few croutons.

Tomato and Fresh Vegetable Gazpacho page 88

Eddie Merlot's Chopped Salad page 100

salads and dressings

Spinach Salad with Hot Bacon Dressing

Bibb Salad with Champagne Vinaigrette

Southwestern Chicken Caesar Salad

Bacon Lettuce and Tomato Salad

MAKES 4-6 SERVINGS

¼ pound bacon

1 cup red onion, sliced

1 cup fresh heirloom tomatoes, diced

2 large heads iceberg lettuce, shredded

1 cup pepper jack cheese, shredded

½ cup hard boiled egg, chopped

½ cup celery, chopped

Ranch Dressing, page 104, or Balsamic Herb Dressing, page 92

Crispy Fried Onions, page 100

Kosher salt

Black pepper

Cut bacon into 1 inch pieces. Heat a medium sauté pan over medium high heat and cook the bacon until all fat is rendered and bacon is crispy. Add the red onion, toss until well coated and remove from the heat. Set bacon and onion mixture aside. Combine the tomatoes, lettuce, pepper jack cheese, egg and celery in a large salad bowl and toss with enough dressing to lightly coat lettuce. Season with salt and pepper. Gently warm the bacon and onion mixture and pour over the top of the salad. Top with fried onions.

Balsamic Herb Vinaigrette Dressing

MAKES 2¼ CUPS

1 tablespoon vegetable oil

2 tablespoons shallots, chopped

1 teaspoon garlic, minced

1 bay leaf

⅛ teaspoon dried thyme leaves

⅛ teaspoon Herbs de Provence

⅛ teaspoon dried basil leaves

Pinch crushed red pepper

1 tablespoon Dijon mustard

½ cup balsamic vinegar

1 tablespoon honey

1 tablespoon sugar

1 ⅔ cups extra virgin olive oil

Black pepper

Kosher salt

In a small sauté pan, sauté the shallots and garlic in the vegetable oil until soft, about 2-3 minutes. Add the bay leaf, thyme, Herbs de Provence and crushed red pepper to the pan and stir until hot. Remove from heat and allow to cool to room temperature. Place cooled herb mixture in a food processor with the Dijon mustard, balsamic vinegar, honey and sugar and puree until smooth. With the motor still running, slowly drizzle in the olive oil in a thin and continuous stream. Season liberally with salt and pepper. Chill dressing for one hour before serving.

Beefsteak Tomato and Onion Salad

MAKES 3-4 SERVINGS

4-6 romaine leaves

2 large beef steak tomatoes

1 small red onion

¾ cup Steak House Bleu Cheese Dressing, page 108

¼ cup bleu cheese crumbles

Cracked black pepper

Wash and dry the romaine leaves and tear them into large pieces. Wash the tomatoes, core and slice each into 4 slices. Peel and slice the red onion into 7 slices. Put the romaine leaves on a large platter and top with the sliced tomatoes and the sliced onions, alternating slices of each. Pour the dressing over the top of the salad and top with the bleu cheese crumbles and a generous amount of cracked black pepper.

This is a classic steak house salad that has been on our menu since the first day. Many a chef has tried to change it, but it's one of those classics you don't mess with.

Beefsteak Tomato and Onion Salad page 92

Bibb Salad with Champagne Vinaigrette

MAKES 3-4 SERVINGS

2 heads bibb lettuce

½ cup hearts of palm, drained and rinsed

¾ cup Champagne Vinaigrette, page 96

½ cup bacon, cooked and chopped

12 grape tomatoes

12 avocado slices

½ cup pistachios, toasted

¼ cup red onion, minced

Cracked black pepper

Wash and dry lettuce. Cut out core, leaving the heads intact. Dice the hearts of palm into ½" pieces. Place the lettuce on a large platter and pour half the dressing over the salad. Evenly top salad with the rest of the ingredients and pour the remaining dressing over the top. Finish with the cracked black pepper.

> Hearts of Palm are just what it says, the inner core of certain palm trees, the most notable being the coconut tree. Harvesting them is a very laborious task, thus classifying them as a delicacy and also explaining their sometimes steep price.

Blackened Prime Steak Salad

MAKES 4 SERVINGS

1 16-ounce prime New York strip steak

1 teaspoon olive oil

1 tablespoon Blackened Spice, page 178

2 heads iceberg head lettuce

½ cup grape tomatoes

½ cup hard boiled eggs, chopped

¼ cup cooked bacon, chopped

½ cup kalamata olives, pitted

1 cup Ranch Dressing, page 104

½ cup Pickled Red Onions, page 102

2 cups Crispy Fried Onions, page 100

Rub the steak with the olive oil and coat all sides with Blackened Spice. Pre-heat grill to high. Grill steak on high until well charred on both sides and medium rare, about 5 minutes per side. Remove from grill and allow to rest while making the salad. Clean and core iceberg lettuce and cut each head into fourths. Place the lettuce wedges on a serving platter and top with the grape tomatoes, chopped egg, chopped bacon and olives. Pour the Ranch Dressing over the salad. Slice the blackened steak thinly on the bias and shingle over the salad. Top with the pickled onions and Crispy Fried Onions.

Caesar Salad with Homemade Croutons

MAKES 3-4 SERVINGS

1 pound romaine hearts

2 cups Caesar Salad Croutons

1 ounce Parmesan cheese, shredded

¾ cup Caesar Salad Dressing, page 96

Wash and dry the romaine hearts and cut into 1" pieces. Place lettuce into a mixing bowl and toss with ½ of the croutons, ½ of the cheese and all of the dressing. Put salad into a serving bowl and top with the remaining croutons and Parmesan cheese.

Caesar Salad Croutons

MAKES 4-6 SERVINGS

1 loaf foccacia bread or other sturdy bread type

Eddie's Bread Seasoning, page 180

Clarified Butter, page 172

Kosher salt

Black pepper

Cut the bread into bite-size pieces and allow to sit in a dry place, uncovered, overnight. The next day preheat oven to 375 degrees. In a large mixing bowl toss the dried bread cubes with enough clarified butter to lightly coat. Toss in some bread seasoning, also until lightly coated. Liberally season with salt and pepper. Toast in the oven until golden brown, about 10-12 minutes.

Blackened Prime Steak Salad page 94

Caesar Salad Dressing

MAKES 2½ CUPS

1 large egg yolk

3 anchovy fillets

⅓ cup red wine vinegar

4 teaspoons white vinegar

2½ tablespoons fresh lemon juice

4-5 roasted garlic cloves

2 teaspoons dry mustard

2-3 drops Tabasco sauce

½ teaspoon Worcestershire sauce

1⅔ cups extra virgin olive oil

2 tablespoons Parmesan cheese, grated

Kosher salt

Black pepper

Combine the egg yolk and anchovies in a food processor and puree for 2 minutes. Turn off motor and add vinegars, lemon juice, roasted garlic, dry mustard, Tabasco and Worcestershire sauce. Puree on high and slowly add the olive oil in a thin and continuous stream. Fold in the Parmesan cheese, season with salt and pepper and pulse to combine. Chill dressing for one hour before serving.

Candied Pecans

MAKES 2 CUPS

½ pound pecan halves

¼ teaspoon cayenne pepper

¼ teaspoon ground cumin

½ teaspoon ground cinnamon

2½ tablespoons Clarified Butter, page 172

3¼ tablespoons brown sugar, lightly packed

½ teaspoon kosher salt

2 teaspoons water

Preheat oven to 375 degrees. In a mixing bowl, thoroughly mix all ingredients together. Spread out pecans evenly on a cookie sheet and bake pecans for 10 minutes. Stir and continue to bake for about 5 more minutes. Pecans should be golden brown and all sugar should be melted and starting to caramelize. Allow pecans to cool to room temperature and break into individual pieces. Store pecans in an airtight container in a cool place away from humidity.

Champagne Vinaigrette

MAKES 2 CUPS

4 teaspoons Dijon mustard

⅓ cup rice vinegar

1 large shallot, minced

1 tablespoon honey

1¼ cups extra virgin olive oil

½ cup champagne

Kosher salt

Black pepper

2 teaspoons fresh tarragon, minced (optional)

Place the mustard, rice vinegar, shallot and honey in a food processor and puree on high for 1 minute. With the motor running slowly add about ½ cup olive oil, then ½ cup champagne, then the rest of the olive oil followed by the remaining champagne. Season liberally with salt and pepper and fold in the tarragon if using. Chill dressing for one hour before serving.

Candied Bacon

MAKES 1 POUND

1 pound thick cut bacon, sliced

1 cup brown sugar

½ teaspoon cayenne pepper

Line the bottom of a sheet pan with parchment paper and top with a roasting rack. Lay the bacon slices in a single layer on top of the rack. In a small mixing bowl, mix the brown sugar and cayenne pepper together. Evenly coat the bacon in the brown sugar mixture. Bake the bacon in a 350 degree oven for 12-15 minutes, rotate pan and continue to cook in 2-3 minute increments until bacon is dark brown, bubbly and crisp. Remove bacon from oven and allow to cool for a few minutes. Transfer to a parchment lined tray while still warm. Serve at room temperature.

Bibb Salad with Champagne Vinaigrette page 96

Crab Louie Salad

MAKES 3-4 SERVINGS

2 heads romaine hearts

1 tomato, thickly sliced

8 cucumber slices

6 red onion slices

½ cup hard boiled egg, chopped

Kosher salt

Black pepper

¾ cup Crab Louie Dressing

¾ pound crab meat, fresh picked

8-12 large shrimp, cooked

¼ cup kalamata olives

Wash and dry the romaine hearts and cut into 1" pieces. Place chopped romaine into a serving bowl. Top the lettuce with the sliced tomatoes, sliced cucumber, sliced red onions and hard boiled egg. Season salad with salt and pepper. Pour the dressing over the salad and finish by topping with the crab meat, shrimp and olives.

This is a very popular salad from our lunch menu that we serve during the holidays. The dressing compliments the sweetness of the crab and brings an elegant balance to the salad.

Crab Louie Salad Dressing

MAKES 2 CUPS

¼ cup green peppers, seeded and chopped

¼ cup green olives, chopped

2 tablespoons green onions, chopped

1½ teaspoons fresh lemon juice

¼ cup heavy cream

1 cup mayonnaise

¼ cup chili sauce

¼ cup ketchup

1 teaspoon Old Bay seasoning

½ teaspoon Tabasco sauce

Kosher salt

Black pepper

Place green peppers, olives, green onion and the lemon juice in a food processor and pulse 5-6 times until evenly chopped, but still having a chunky texture. Empty contents into a mixing bowl, add the rest of the ingredients, season liberally with salt and pepper and mix well. Chill dressing for at least one hour before serving.

Crab Pasta Salad with Spinach and Artichokes

MAKES 4 SERVINGS

½ cup extra virgin olive oil

½ cup red wine vinegar

¾ teaspoon garlic, minced

¾ teaspoon dried basil leaves

¾ teaspoon dried oregano leaves

¾ teaspoon sugar

3 cups cooked pasta, cook's choice

½ cup grape tomatoes, split in half

1 cup frozen artichoke hearts, thawed and chopped

¼ cup green onion, chopped

2 ounces spinach leaves

¼ pound fresh lump crab meat

¼ teaspoon crushed red pepper

½ teaspoon Old Bay seasoning

Kosher salt

Black pepper

In a large mixing bowl, whisk together the olive oil, red wine vinegar, garlic, basil, oregano and sugar. Fold in the pasta, grape tomatoes, artichokes, green onions, spinach, crab meat, red pepper and Old Bay seasoning. Liberally season with salt and pepper and place in the refrigerator for an hour to chill before serving.

Crab Louie Salad page 98

Creamy French Dressing

MAKES 2¼ CUPS

½ cup vegetable oil

1 tablespoon paprika, heaping

2 egg yolks

1½ teaspoons Dijon mustard

5 tablespoons cider vinegar

1 cup vegetable oil

½ cup brown sugar

⅛ teaspoon white pepper

¼ teaspoon garlic powder

¼ teaspoon kosher salt

2 whole eggs, beaten

Day before: make the paprika oil by gently warming the first measurement of vegetable oil with the paprika to about 100 degrees, over low heat. Cover and allow to sit at room temperature overnight.

Day of preparation: combine egg yolks, mustard and cider vinegar in a food processor and puree on high. With the motor running, slowly drizzle in the vegetable oil in a thin, continuous stream. With the motor still running, repeat the process with the paprika flavored oil, making sure to incorporate any paprika that has settled to the bottom of the container. Stop the motor and mix in the brown sugar, white pepper, garlic powder and salt. Scrape down the sides and bottom with a rubber spatula. Pulse mixer until ingredients are well combined. Chill dressing 1-2 hours before serving.

Crispy Fried Onions

MAKES 4 SERVINGS

1 cup flour

1 tablespoon corn starch

1¼ teaspoons kosher salt

1¼ teaspoons ground cumin

¾ teaspoon cayenne pepper

1¼ teaspoons paprika

¾ teaspoon sugar

1¼ teaspoons granulated garlic

1 onion, peeled and shaved

Preheat deep fryer to 350 degrees. In a small bowl, combine the four with the spices and mix thoroughly. Rinse and shake dry the shaved onions and dredge in the seasoned flour. Deep fry onions until golden brown, about 3 minutes. Drain onions and season lightly with kosher salt.

Eddie Merlot's Chopped Salad

MAKES 4-6 SERVINGS

4 ounces romaine lettuce

8 ounces iceberg lettuce

4 ounces radicchio lettuce

¾ cup Gruyere cheese, shredded

¼ cup red onion, minced

½ cup celery, diced

½ cup beefsteak tomato, diced

½ cup hearts of palm, diced

¼ pound prosciutto ham, julienned

¾ cup Eddie Merlot's Creamy Herb Dressing, page 102

¼ cup toasted almonds, sliced

Trim and shred all the lettuces before washing and drying. Place lettuce in a large mixing bowl and toss with the Gruyere cheese, red onion, celery, tomato, hearts of palm, prosciutto ham and the dressing until thoroughly mixed. Place salad into a serving bowl and top with toasted almonds.

The salad portion of our Dinner Menu is in a constant evolution. It has some staples that we dare not touch, Caesar Salad and Tomato Salad, to name two, but the rest change with the dining tastes of our guests. For example, the Spinach Salad started out as a basic steak house spinach salad which was popular 10 years ago. As the popularity died off and guests were looking for something more "exotic", it was removed from our menu. When the trend of comfort food made a comeback, we went to work re-inventing the classic to include strawberries, goat cheese and candied bacon while still using the familiar Hot Bacon Dressing. You will just have to stay tuned to see what the next exciting salad will be!

Bacon Lettuce and Tomato Salad with Crispy Fried Onions page 100

Eddie Merlot's Creamy Herb Dressing

MAKES 2 CUPS

1 egg yolk

1 tablespoon Dijon mustard

¼ cup rice vinegar

¼ cup honey

1 teaspoon dry mustard

1 teaspoon fresh basil, chopped

1 teaspoon fresh chives, chopped

1 teaspoon fresh parsley, chopped

1⅓ cups vegetable oil

Kosher salt

Black pepper

Place egg yolk, Dijon mustard, rice vinegar, honey, dry mustard and herbs in a food processor. Puree on high for 2-3 minutes. With motor running, slowly add the oil. Dressing should be creamy and emulsified. Season liberally with salt and pepper. Chill dressing for one hour before serving.

Garlic Honey Mustard Vinaigrette

MAKES 1½ CUPS

1 tablespoon shallots, chopped

1 teaspoon garlic clove, minced

¼ cup Dijon mustard

¼ cup apple cider vinegar

¼ cup honey

1 cup extra virgin olive oil

1 tablespoon yellow mustard seeds

Kosher salt

Black pepper

Place the shallot, garlic, Dijon mustard, honey and cider vinegar in a food processor and puree on high. With the motor running, slowly add the olive oil in a thin and continuous stream. Season dressing with salt and lots of black pepper and add in the mustard seeds.

This dressing goes very well with the Roasted Beet Salad, page 104, or even tossed with summer vegetables before grilling.

Merlot Iceberg Salad

MAKES 4-6 SERVINGS

2 large heads iceberg lettuce

1 cup Steak House Bleu Cheese Dressing, page 108

12 grape tomatoes

¾ cup hard boiled egg, chopped

¾ cup cooked bacon, chopped

½ cup kalamata olives, pitted

¼ cup Pickled Red Onions

Trim the outer leaves of the lettuce, remove the core and cut each head into fourths. Place iceberg wedges on a serving platter and pour the dressing over the lettuce. Top the salad with the tomatoes, chopped egg, bacon pieces, olives and the pickled onions.

Pickled Red Onions

MAKES 2 CUPS

1 quart water

4-5 cups red onion, peeled and shaved

2 cups rice vinegar

1 cup sugar

1 teaspoon kosher salt

2 fresh thyme sprigs

In a small sauce pan, bring water to a boil. Place the shaved red onion in a strainer over the sink. Pour the boiling water over the onions and allow to drain. In the same sauce pan bring the rice vinegar, sugar and kosher salt to a boil. When the onions have drained, place them in a heat proof storage container. Add the thyme sprigs to the container. Pour the hot vinegar mixture over the onions, stir to coat and allow to marinate in the refrigerator for at least 6-8 hours before serving. Keep refrigerated until serving.

This is a great pickling liquid that you can use for all kinds of vegetables, not just onions. Substituting carrots and jalapeños for the onions makes for a tasty treat with grilled steak tacos.

Merlot Iceberg Salad page 102

Ranch Salad Dressing

MAKES 2 CUPS

2 cups mayonnaise

½ cup buttermilk

2 4-ounce packets Hidden Valley Ranch salad dressing mix

¼ teaspoon fresh lemon juice

2-3 drops Worcestershire sauce

2-3 drops Tabasco sauce

¼ teaspoon black pepper

2 whole eggs, beaten

Place all ingredients in food processor and pulse until thoroughly combined. Chill for one hour before serving.

This is a basic ranch dressing recipe. We have played with different recipes in the past, but our clientele and staff always come back to this one. Something about the classics that you just shouldn't mess with.

Red Wine Vinaigrette

MAKES 2 CUPS

4 anchovies, rinsed

¾ teaspoon dried oregano leaves

1 tablespoon fresh basil leaves, minced

1 tablespoon shallots, diced

5 tablespoons red wine vinegar

3 tablespoons red wine

4 teaspoons sugar

2½ tablespoons corn starch

¾ teaspoon crushed red pepper

2½ tablespoon Parmesan cheese, grated

1⅓ cups extra virgin olive oil

Kosher salt

Black pepper

Measure all of the ingredients except the olive oil into a food processor and puree on high for 2-3 minutes. With the motor running, slowly drizzle in the olive oil in a thin and continuous stream. Season with salt and pepper. Chill for one hour before serving.

This is also a great dressing for a Grilled Chicken Caesar Salad.

Roasted Beet and Goat Cheese Salad

MAKES 3-4 SERVINGS

1 pound whole beets, assorted colors

1 teaspoon olive oil

Kosher salt

8 slices prosciutto ham

2 oranges

3 heads frisee lettuce, washed and trimmed

½ cup walnuts, lightly toasted

2 tablespoons fresh basil, chopped

½ cup Garlic Honey Mustard Vinaigrette, page 102

3 ounces goat cheese, crumbled

Preheat oven to 375 degrees. Peel and dice beets into 1 inch cubes. Toss beets with the olive oil and season liberally with salt and pepper. Roast beets on a cooking sheet for about 40 minutes, until beets are tender and caramelized. Set aside. Turn on the broiler. Lay the prosciutto ham slices flat on a cookie sheet wrapped in tin foil and broil ham for 2-3 minutes on both sides until golden brown. Remove from oven and allow to cool. The slices will continue to crisp as they cool. Peel the oranges and cut into segments. In a large mixing bowl toss the oranges with the frisee lettuce, toasted walnuts, chopped basil and the Garlic Honey Mustard Vinaigrette. Transfer salad to a serving bowl and top with the roasted beets and goat cheese. Cut the crispy ham into thin strips and lay on top of the salad for garnish.

Roasted Beet and Goat Cheese Salad page 104

Romaine Waldorf Salad

MAKES 3-4 SERVINGS

2 heads romaine lettuce

1 Granny Smith apple

1 cup red seedless grapes

¾ cup Maple-Cider Vinaigrette

¼ cup bleu cheese crumbles

½ cup Candied Pecans, page 96

1 tablespoon chives, chopped

Split the romaine heads in half, wash and shake dry. Cut the cores out, leaving the lettuce whole. Put the romaine heads, cut side up, on a large platter. Core and thinly slice the apple and place on top of the lettuce. Add the grapes to the salad and pour the dressing evenly over the lettuce. Top salad with the bleu cheese crumbles, Candied Pecans and the chopped chives.

Maple-Cider Vinaigrette

MAKES 2 CUPS

2 tablespoons Dijon mustard

½ cup apple cider vinegar

1 small shallot, minced

½ cup real maple syrup

1½ cups extra virgin olive oil

Kosher salt

Black pepper

Spinach Salad with Hot Bacon Dressing

MAKES 4-6 SERVINGS

½ pound fresh spinach, stems removed

½ cup hard boiled egg, chopped

¾ cup strawberries, sliced

½ cup goat cheese, crumbled

¼ cup crisp bacon pieces

¾ cup Hot Bacon Dressing

8 red onion rings

4 Candied Bacon slices, page 96

Wash and dry spinach and place in a large mixing bowl. Heat the bacon dressing until hot. Toss the spinach with the chopped egg, strawberries, goat cheese and bacon pieces. Pour hot dressing over salad and toss to coat. Put salad in a serving bowl and top with red onion rings and the Candied Bacon. Serve immediately.

Place the Dijon mustard, vinegar and shallot in a food processor and puree until smooth. With the motor running add half the olive oil in a thin continuous stream. Add half the maple syrup, then the rest of the olive oil, followed by the remaining maple syrup. Season with salt and pepper and blend for 2 minutes. Chill for an hour before serving.

Spinach Salad Hot Bacon Dressing

MAKES 1½ CUPS

6 ounces bacon, medium dice

1 cup bacon grease

⅓ cup yellow onions, minced

¾ cup red wine vinegar

½ cup water

½ cup sugar

Kosher salt

Black pepper

2 teaspoons water

2 teaspoons corn starch

In a medium sauce pan, render the bacon until crispy. Strain out bacon, set aside, reserving one cup of bacon grease. Return the bacon grease to the sauce pan and sauté the onions until soft. Add the red wine vinegar, ½ cup water and sugar and bring to a boil. Reduce heat to a simmer. In a small mixing bowl, mix 2 teaspoons water with the corn starch and whisk smooth to form a paste or slurry. Whisk slurry into the simmering liquid and continue to cook on low for 6-7 minutes. Remove dressing from heat, liberally season with salt and pepper and stir in the reserved bacon. Serve hot with spinach salad.

Spinach Salad with Hot Bacon Dressing page 106

Southwestern Chicken Caesar Salad

MAKES 3-4 SERVINGS

1 pound romaine lettuce

4 ounces red cabbage, shredded

1 pound boneless chicken thighs

3 ears fresh sweet corn

1 teaspoon extra virgin olive oil

Kosher salt

Black pepper

1 cup cooked black beans

1 cup grape tomatoes, halved

1 cup jicama, peeled and ½" diced

1 cup pepper jack cheese, shredded

¾ cup Southwestern Caesar Dressing

½ cup tortilla chips, crushed

2 tablespoons fresh cilantro, chopped

Preheat grill to high. While grill is heating, cut romaine heads into bite-size pieced, wash and dry and place into a large mixing bowl with the red cabbage. Rub chicken thighs and corn on the cob with olive oil and season with salt and pepper. Grill both until chicken is done and the corn is tender with good char marks. Set aside to cool. Toss lettuce mixture with black beans, tomatoes, jicama and jack cheese. Remove corn kernels from the cob, dice the chicken into bite-size pieces and add both to the lettuce mixture. Add dressing, tortilla chips and cilantro and toss until well coated. Serve immediately.

Southwestern Caesar Salad Dressing

MAKES 3-4 SERVINGS

1¾ cup Caesar Salad Dressing, page 96

1 chipotle pepper (canned en adobo)

1 tablespoon fresh cilantro, chopped

2 tablespoons green onion, sliced

1½ teaspoon Blackened Spice, page 178

1 teaspoon ground cumin

1¾ tablespoons balsamic vinegar

3 ounces pepper jack cheese, grated

¾ teaspoon dried basil leaves

Kosher salt

Black pepper

Measure all ingredients together into a food processor and puree on high until smooth, 3-4 minutes. Season with salt and pepper. Chill dressing one hour before serving.

The original Caesar salad is said to have originated in Tijuana, Mexico. So, the next logical evolution of flavors would be to add chipotle peppers, cilantro and cumin which is just what we did to update the classic salad into something very unique.

Steak House Bleu Cheese Dressing

MAKES 4 CUPS

1⅓ cups mayonnaise

¾ cup sour cream

1½ tablespoon red wine vinegar

⅓ cup buttermilk

1 teaspoon Worcestershire sauce

¼ teaspoon Tabasco sauce

½ teaspoon dry mustard

Pinch cayenne pepper

10 ounces bleu cheese, crumbled

Kosher salt

Black pepper

Combine all ingredients and half the bleu cheese in a food processor and puree on high until smooth. Pour dressing into a mixing bowl and fold in the remaining bleu cheese crumbles and season with salt and pepper. Chill dressing one hour before serving.

Bleu Cheese Dressing is a staple at every great American steak house. What separates ours from the pack is blending some of the cheese in the base of the dressing for flavor and then folding in chunks for texture at the end. The result is a decadently rich dressing that is both creamy and chunky that will satisfy even the most critical Bleu Cheese Dressing connoisseur.

Southwestern Chicken Caesar Salad page 108

Strawberry-Poppy Seed Dressing

MAKES 1½ CUPS

¼   pound fresh strawberries

¼   cup red wine vinegar

½   cup sugar

1   tablespoon dry mustard

½   cup extra virgin olive oil

1½   tablespoons poppy seed

Kosher salt

Black pepper

Rinse and de-stem strawberries and combine in a food processor with the red wine vinegar, sugar and dry mustard. Puree on high until smooth. With motor running, slowly drizzle the olive oil in a steady and continuous stream. Add poppy seeds and season with salt and pepper and pulse to combine. Chill dressing one hour before serving.

Although this dressing is great on just about any salad, it is particularly good on a spinach salad with roasted pears, fresh goat cheese and toasted pumpkin seeds. We have even used it as a dressing for fruit salad on a brunch buffet.

Tuscan Grilled Panzanella Salad

MAKES 4-6 SERVINGS

1   loaf French style bread

Olive oil

Kosher salt

Black pepper

¼   cup heirloom tomatoes, ½" diced

¼   cup fresh mozzarella cheese, ½" diced

¼   cup cucumber, ½" diced

¼   cup red onion, ½" diced

2   tablespoons capers

½   cup frozen artichoke hearts, thawed

¼   cup nicoise olives

4   cups radicchio lettuce, shredded

4   cups frisee lettuce

¾   cup Red Wine Vinaigrette, page 104

3-ounce chunk Parmesan cheese

2   tablespoons fresh chives, minced

Day before: preheat grill to high. Cut French bread into 1" thick slices and brush liberally with olive oil. Season with salt and pepper and grill until evenly charred on both sides, but not burned. Set aside, uncovered, to dry overnight.

Day of preparation: cut enough of the grilled bread slices into 1" chunks to get 4 cups. In a large mixing bowl toss bread cubes with tomatoes, mozzarella, cucumbers, red onion, capers, artichoke hearts, olives, radicchio, frisee and Red Wine Vinaigrette. Season with salt and pepper and mix well. Use a vegetable peeler to shave the Parmesan cheese over the salad and top with chopped chives.

Tuscan Turkey Salad

MAKES 6-8 SERVINGS

1   red pepper

1   small red onion, peeled

1½   cups frozen artichoke hearts, thawed

¼   cup whole almonds

¾   cup assorted olives, pitted

2   pounds roasted turkey breast, diced

½   cup red onion, sliced

2   tablespoons fresh basil, chopped

2   tablespoons fresh parsley, chopped

⅓   cup extra virgin olive oil

½   fresh lemon, zested

1   tablespoon balsamic vinegar

¼   teaspoon crushed red pepper

Kosher salt

Black pepper

Preheat oven to 375 degrees. Chop red pepper into 1" cubes and quarter the whole red onion. Toss the pepper and red onion with the artichoke hearts, almond and olives with a touch of olive oil. Season with salt and pepper and place on a baking tray. Bake in the oven for 20-25 minutes until vegetables are soft and beginning to brown. Transfer ingredients to a mixing bowl and toss with the rest of the ingredients. Season with salt and pepper.

This is a great salad to make using left-over Thanksgiving turkey. You don't have to wait until then, however. Just roast a turkey breast the night before and toss it all together the next day for a great lunch. In this salad we combined roasted and raw onions to give contrasting tastes and textures.

Tuscan Turkey Salad page 110

Grilled Bison Filet page 120

entrees

Beef, Pork, Veal, Lamb and Game

Braised Pork Osso Bucco

Poultry

Meyer Lemon Chicken

Seafood

Barbecue Glazed Cedar Plank Salmon

Beef Bourguignon over Buttered Noodles

MAKES 8-10 SERVINGS

- 2 tablespoons olive oil
- ½ pound bacon, cut in 1" pieces
- 2½ pounds beef tips, trimmed and cut in 1" chunks
- 1 pound carrots, peeled, sliced diagonally into 1" chunks
- 2 small onions, peeled and sliced
- 1 tablespoon garlic, chopped
- ½ cup cognac
- 4 cups burgundy wine
- 2 cups Beef Stock, page 52
- 2 tablespoons tomato paste
- 1 teaspoon fresh thyme, chopped
- 1 bay leaf
- 2 tablespoons Clarified Butter, page 172
- 3 tablespoons flour
- ¾ pound cippollini onions, peeled and cut into fourths
- ½ pound Roasted Mushrooms, page 164
- Kosher salt and black pepper
- 2 pounds buttered noodles, cooked

In a large stock pot, brown bacon in oil until slightly crispy; remove from pot. Sear beef in hot grease until golden and remove. Sauté onion and carrots in the hot grease, lower heat and cook until onions are golden. Add garlic and deglaze pot with cognac. Add bacon, beef, wine, Beef Stock, tomato paste, thyme and bay leaf. Bring stew to a low simmer, cover and cook for one hour until beef is tender. Make a roux with butter and flour and whisk into the stew. Add onions and mushrooms. Continue to simmer for 15 more minutes. Season with salt and pepper and serve over buttered noodles.

Bourbon Marinated Pork Chops

MAKES 7 SERVINGS

- 1 whole, 7 bone pork rack
- 2 quarts Bourbon and Brown Sugar Brine, page 54
- Steak Seasoning, page 180
- 1 cup Southern Comfort Peach Barbecue Sauce, page 44

Place pork rack into a Tupperware style container with a tight-fitting lid. Pour the Bourbon and Brown Sugar Brine over the rack, cover with the lid and allow to marinate at least 3 days in the refrigerator. If the brine does not fully submerge the rack, flip rack every 12 hours during the brining time. Preheat oven to 300 degrees. Remove pork rack from brine and pat dry with paper towels. Discard brine. Put pork on a roasting rack and place in the oven until an internal temperature of 100 degrees is achieved. Remove pork rack from oven and allow to cool to room temperature. When cool, place pork in the refrigerator overnight or for at least six hours. Preheat grill to medium high. Cut pork rack into 7 individual chops and season liberally with the Steak Seasoning and place on the grill. Grill for 4-5 minutes on one side, flip and brush with barbecue sauce and continue to cook for another 5-6 minutes. Flip, brush with barbecue sauce and repeat process until pork chops are caramelized, about 20 minutes total.

Bourbon Marinated Ribeye Steak

MAKES 4-6 SERVINGS

- 4 12-ounce prime ribeye steaks
- 1½ cups Kentucky Bourbon Steak Marinade, page 56
- Steak Seasoning, page 180
- 2 tablespoons Steak Butter, page 176

Place the ribeyes into a 1 gallon sealable bag. Add the bourbon marinade, squeeze out the air and seal. Place the bag into a baking dish and place in the bottom of the refrigerator for at least 12 hours, preferably 24. At the restaurant we marinate for 48 hours. Preheat grill to medium high. Remove steaks from the marinade and pat dry with paper towels. Discard used marinade. Season steaks with the Steak Seasoning. Grill to desired temperature, about 6-7 minutes per side for medium rare. Remove steaks from the grill and brush with the Steak Butter before serving.

This is one of our most popular signature steaks. It is also one of the most requested recipes by our guests. We regularly get calls from guests who want to replicate this steak at home. So this is the recipe that we have been, up till now, very tight lipped about. We hope you enjoy!

Beef Bourguignon over Buttered Noodles page 114

Braised Beef Short Ribs

MAKES 6 SERVINGS

6 beef short ribs, 24-ounce, 3 bone

Kosher salt

Black pepper

6 tablespoons Clarified Butter, page 172

3 carrots, cut in large chunks

3 stalks celery, cut in large chunks

1 small onion, quartered

1 tablespoon garlic, minced

3 tablespoons tomato paste

2 bay leaves

6 fresh thyme sprigs

1 fresh rosemary sprig

4 cups Beef Stock, page 52

2 cups red wine

Preheat oven to 325 degrees. Place a roasting pan over medium high heat. Season the ribs with salt and pepper. Add the Clarified Butter to the roasting pan and sear the ribs until golden brown on both sides. Remove the ribs from the pan and place on a cooling rack. Add the carrots, celery, onion, garlic, tomato paste, bay leaves, thyme and rosemary sprigs to the pan. Cook for 2-3 minutes until vegetables start to color. Add the Beef Stock and the red wine. Place the reserved short ribs in the pan and cover with parchment paper and foil and bake for 2½ - 3 hours. Check for tenderness. Meat should pull from the bone. If not done, check in 20 minute intervals until done. Remove from oven and strain cooking liquid into a small sauce pan. Remove fat from the top of the liquid, bring liquid to a boil and reduce by 50%. Taste and season with salt and pepper, strain again and serve with ribs.

Braised Pork Osso Bucco

MAKES 6-8 SERVINGS

6 fresh pork shanks, 16-ounces each

Kosher salt

Black pepper

4 tablespoons Clarified Butter, page 172

6 fresh thyme sprigs

5 fresh parsley sprigs

2 fresh rosemary sprigs

2 cups white wine

3 carrots, cut in large chunks

3 stalks celery, cut in large chunks

1 small onion, quartered

1 tablespoon garlic, minced

3 tablespoons tomato paste

2 bay leaves

2 ½ cups Beef Stock, page 52

Preheat oven to 325 degrees. Liberally season pork shanks with salt and pepper. In a large skillet, working in batches, sear the pork shanks in the Clarified Butter until golden brown on all sides. Using butcher's twine, tie the thyme, rosemary and parsley sprigs together into a bundle. Place the herb bundle and the rest of the ingredients into a roasting pan or Dutch oven. Place the Osso Bucco on top of the vegetables in the roasting pan or Dutch oven and cover with parchment paper and foil. Bake for 3 hours or until fork tender. Remove roasting pan from oven and allow Osso Bucco to cool in the liquid for about 30 minutes. Strain braising liquid and reduce by about 50%. Strain again, season sauce with salt and pepper and serve with the shanks.

Chimichurri Pork Chops with Pineapple Salsa

MAKES 4 SERVINGS

4 8-ounce boneless pork chops, 1" thick

8 tablespoons Chimichurri Sauce, page 30

3 tablespoons rice vinegar

1½ tablespoons brown sugar

¼ teaspoon ground cumin

⅓ cup red onion, minced

1½ cups fresh pineapple, cored and diced

⅓ cup red pepper, diced

2 teaspoons jalapeño, minced

2 teaspoons honey

2 teaspoons fresh cilantro, chopped

Kosher salt

Black pepper

4-5 fresh cilantro sprigs

Toss the pork chops with 4 tablespoons Chimichurri Sauce and let sit at room temperature for an hour. While chops are sitting, make the pineapple-jalapeño salsa by combining the vinegar, sugar and cumin together in a sauce pan and place over medium heat. Stir until sugar has completely dissolved. Remove from heat and allow to cool fully. In a glass mixing bowl, fold together the rest of the ingredients, except cilantro sprigs, season with salt and pepper and fold in the cooled vinegar/spice mixture and mix well. Pre-heat grill to medium high and grill pork chops until evenly charred on both sides and still rosy pink inside, about 5-6 minutes per side. Place the pineapple salsa on a large serving tray and top with the pork chops. Spoon the remaining 4 tablespoons of the Chimichurri Sauce over the chops and garnish with the cilantro sprigs.

Braised Beef Short Ribs page 116

Coffee Crusted Lamb with Mint Pesto

MAKES 3-4 SERVINGS

8 6-ounce lamb rib chops

Coffee Rub, page 180

Mint Pesto

Asparagus and Potato Risotto, page 156

Preheat grill to medium. Liberally crust the lamb chops with the Coffee Rub and set aside. Make pesto and set aside. Grill the lamb chops for 4-5 minutes each side for medium rare. Place the lamb chops on a serving platter and spoon the mint pesto over the chops. Serve with the Asparagus and Potato Risotto.

Mint Pesto

1½ cups fresh mint leaves, loosely packed

½ cup macadamia nuts, toasted

¾ cup extra virgin olive oil

1 teaspoon lemon zest

2 tablespoons Parmesan cheese, grated

Kosher salt

Black pepper

Put the mint leaves and macadamia nuts in a food processor and puree until smooth. With the motor running, slowly drizzle in the olive oil until fully incorporated. Add the lemon zest, Parmesan cheese, season with salt and pepper and pulse to combine. Wrap tightly and set aside. Makes 1 cup.

Dijon Elk Chop with Fennel Mushroom Sauce

MAKES 4 SERVINGS

1 small head fresh fennel

Olive oil

4 8-ounce elk rack chops

1 tablespoon Dijon mustard

Steak Seasoning, page 180

2 tablespoons Clarified Butter, page 172

1 cup crimini mushrooms, quartered

¼ cup cabernet wine

¾ cup Steak Diane Sauce, page 46

Eddie's Garlic Mashed Potatoes, page 160

4 fresh rosemary sprigs

Preheat oven to 350 degrees. Rub fennel with a touch of olive oil and place into a small baking dish. Place in the oven for 1 hour until soft. Remove from oven and cool. Brush the elk chops with the Dijon mustard and season with the Steak Seasoning. In a large sauté skillet, heat the Clarified Butter over medium high heat. When hot, add the elk chops and sear until golden brown, about 3-4 minutes. Flip chops and transfer the whole skillet to the oven and cook for 10-12 minutes for medium rare. Remove the skillet from the oven, remove chops from the pan and drain any excess grease from the pan. Dice the roasted fennel into 1 inch pieces and add to the pan along with the crimini mushrooms. Deglaze pan with the wine and cook for 2-3 minutes. Add the Diane Sauce to the pan; reduce heat to low and cook until mushrooms are soft, about 6-7 minutes. Place a generous scoop of potatoes onto four dinner plates. Lean an elk chop against the potatoes and spoon the mushroom/fennel sauce around the elk. Garnish each plate with a rosemary sprig.

Eddie's Classic Grilled Filet Mignon

MAKES 4 SERVINGS

4 8-ounce prime filet mignons

Steak Seasoning, page 180

4 teaspoons Steak Butter, page 176

Eddie's Garlic Mashed Potatoes, page 160

Creamed Spinach, page 160

Preheat grill to high. Season steaks liberally with the Steak Seasoning and set at room temperature for 1 hour. Grill steaks over the hottest part of the grill until a nice charred crust has formed on both sides. Move steaks to a lower temperature spot to finish cooking to desired temperature. It will be in the neighborhood of 6-7 minutes per side total for medium rare, depending on the size and temperature range of your grill. Remove the steaks and place on a serving platter and brush with the steak butter. Allow to sit for 8-10 minutes before cutting. Serve with the mashed potatoes and the Creamed Spinach.

This is the recipe! This is what we have built our reputation on. It is our #1 selling dish and is what all others are measured against. We suggest trying the mashed potatoes and the creamed spinach with your steaks, which are two of our best selling sides, to complete the experience.

Eddie's Classic Grilled Filet Mignon page 118

Filet and Lobster Wellington

MAKES 4 SERVINGS

4 8-ounce prime filet mignons

Steak Seasoning, page 180

2 teaspoons olive oil

1 sheet puff pastry, thawed

¼ cup Roasted Mushrooms, page 164

1 12-ounce lobster tail, cooked

1 egg, lightly beaten

1 cup Burgundy Wine Sauce, page 28

1 cup Traditional Béarnaise Sauce, page 48

Preheat grill to 400 degrees. Season the filets with the Steak Seasoning. Heat the olive oil in a medium skillet over medium high heat and sear the filets until golden brown on both sides and just barely cooked inside, about 2-3 minutes per side. Remove steaks from the pan and pat dry. Lay the puff pastry sheet on a cutting board and cut into 4 equal squares. Finely dice the roasted mushrooms and divide evenly in the center of each puff pastry square. Slice the lobster tail into 4 equal slices and place one slice on top of the mushrooms. Place the now cooled filets on top of each mushroom lobster mixture. Fold each corner of the puff pastry up over the filets to create a package. Flip, seam side down, on a baking tray and brush wellingtons evenly with the egg wash. Place the wellingtons in the oven for about 20-25 minutes until pastry is an even golden brown. Remove from oven. Gently heat the Burgundy Wine Sauce and spoon on the bottom of four dinner plates. Put the wellingtons on top of the wine sauce and serve with the Béarnaise Sauce on the side.

Filet Trio of Medallions

MAKES 4 SERVINGS

12 4-ounce prime filet mignons

Steak Seasoning, page 180

4 tablespoons Bacon and Gorgonzola Cheese Crust, page 26

1 tablespoon olive oil

¼ pound lump crab meat

12 fresh asparagus spears, blanched

½ cup Traditional Béarnaise Sauce, page 48

½ cup Peppercorn Sauce, page 40

Preheat grill to high. Season filets with the steak seasoning and grill until desired temperature, about 4-5 minutes per side for medium rare. Remove from grill. Top four of the medallions with one tablespoon each of the bacon and gorgonzola cheese crust and place under a broiler until golden brown. In a small sauté pan, warm the crab meat in the olive oil, add the blanched asparagus, toss until hot and season with salt and pepper. Plate two of the medallions on one of four dinner plates with a cheese crusted medallion. Divide the crab and asparagus mixture among one filet on each plate and top with two tablespoons of Béarnaise Sauce. Ladle two tablespoons Peppercorn Sauce over the remaining 4 medallions. Each plate should have one medallion with cheese crust, one medallion with crabmeat, asparagus and Béarnaise Sauce and one medallion with Peppercorn Sauce.

Grilled Bison Filet

MAKES 4 SERVINGS

4 8-ounce bison filets

1 teaspoon extra virgin olive oil

Steak Seasoning, page 180

½ pound fingerling potatoes, split lengthwise

3 tablespoons Clarified Butter, page 172

1 cup fresh brussels sprouts, split in half

8 small cippollini onions, peeled

¾ cup Steak Diane Sauce, page 46

2 teaspoons fresh chives, chopped

Kosher salt

Black pepper

Preheat oven to 375 degrees. Rub bison steaks with olive oil and season with Steak Seasoning. Set steaks aside. Toss fingerling potatoes with a touch of olive oil and season with salt and pepper. Place on a cookie sheet and roast in the oven until tender, about 35 minutes. While potatoes are roasting, heat the Clarified Butter until hot and add the brussels sprouts and onions, season with salt and pepper, reduce heat to medium low and continue to cook until mixture is golden brown and vegetables are soft, about 10-12 minutes. Preheat grill to high. Grill bison filets over very high heat for 7-8 minutes on each side for medium rare. Set aside. Toss the roasted fingerling potatoes with the brussels sprouts mixture and place on the bottom of four serving plates. Top each plate with a bison filet. Gently warm the Steak Diane Sauce and spoon around the bison filets and garnish with the chopped chives.

Filet Trio of Medallions page 120

Grilled Cajun Ribeye

MAKES 4 SERVINGS

4 12-ounce prime ribeye steaks

¾ cup Cajun Marinade, page 54

2 tablespoons Chipotle Butter, page 172

In a small mixing bowl toss the steaks with the Cajun Marinade until well coated. Place the steaks in a sealable plastic bag, remove as much air as possible and seal. Place steaks in the refrigerator overnight. Preheat grill to medium high. Remove steaks from the marinade, discard excess marinade and allow steaks to sit at room temperature for 30 minutes. Grill steaks to desired doneness, about 7-8 minutes per side for medium rare, being careful to move steaks from one part of the grill to the other to avoid flare ups. Brush finished steaks with the Chipotle Butter and allow to rest for 5-6 minutes before serving.

Grilled Chipotle Beef Skewers

MAKES 4 SERVINGS

16 2-ounce prime beef tips, cubed

16 pieces onion, large diced

16 pieces red pepper, large diced

16 cherry tomatoes

16 large button mushrooms

4 metal skewers

Kosher salt

Black pepper

½ cup Chipotle Grilling Sauce, page 30

2 tablespoons Chipotle Butter, page 172

Skewer four pieces of meat with four pieces of each vegetable in any pattern you desire. Preheat grill to high. Season skewers with salt and pepper. Place skewers on the hottest part of the grill and brush with the Chipotle Grill Sauce. Grill for 2-3 minutes. Flip skewers and continue to brush with the grill sauce until done, about 4 minutes each side. Place skewers on a serving platter, brush with the Chipotle Butter and serve.

Grilled Veal Chop Dijonnaise

MAKES 4 SERVINGS

4 12-ounce veal rib chops

Steak Seasoning, page 180

6 slices bacon, cut in 1" pieces

12 whole cippollini onions, peeled and cut in half

2 cups button mushrooms, split in half

½ cup white wine

8 cups Steak Diane Sauce, page 46

1 teaspoon fresh parsley, chopped

Preheat grill to medium high. Season the veal chops with the Steak Seasoning and grill to desired temperature over medium high heat, about 7 minutes per side for medium. While the chops are cooking, fry the bacon in a medium skillet until crispy. Remove bacon from the pan and reserve. Adjust heat to medium and add the cippollini onions and button mushrooms to the hot bacon grease and cook until mixture is a golden brown. Deglaze pan with the white wine and reduce until almost dry. Add the Steak Diane Sauce and heat until hot. Fold in the reserved crispy bacon pieces and the chopped parsley. Season with salt and pepper. Spoon mushroom/bacon sauce over the veal chops and serve.

You will be surprised by what a little patience, preplanning, and a few simple ingredients can do to change the whole flavor of your next backyard barbecue.

This is a summer cookout classic. Here we have stuck with the basics that work, and elevated the flavors with a grilling sauce and a finishing butter that are made from smoked red jalapeños that make these beef skewers far from ordinary.

Grilled Cajun Ribeye page 122

New Orleans Mixed Grill

MAKES 4 SERVINGS

4 4-ounce prime filet mignons

8 large 8-12 P&D shrimp, raw

4 links andouille sausage, cut in 3" pieces

2 tablespoons olive oil

Blackened Spice, page 178

Andouille Sausage Gravy, page 26

Eddie's Garlic Mashed Potatoes, page 160

Preheat grill to high. In a small mixing bowl toss the filets, shrimp and sausage with the olive oil and liberally season with the Blackened Spice. Gently warm the Andouille Sausage Gravy and keep hot. Place the steaks on the grill and cook to desired temperature. Add the shrimp and sausage and grill until the shrimp is cooked and the sausage is heated through. Put a generous scoop of mashed potatoes on each of four serving plates and top with a filet, 2 shrimp and a sausage link. Spoon ⅓ cup of the sausage gravy over the top of each dish and serve.

> This recipe was inspired by a trip to New Orleans where all of the menus seemed to be dominated by a robust, smoky, slightly spicy pork and potato sausage called andouille. This is our tribute of sorts to the true king of pork sausage.

Sautéed Pork Tenderloin with Red Eye Gravy

MAKES 4-6 SERVINGS

2 1¼ pound pork tenderloins, trimmed

2 teaspoons whole grain mustard

6 thin slices prosciutto ham

Kosher salt

Black pepper

1 tablespoon Clarified Butter, page 172

½ cup strong coffee

½ cup Beef Stock, page 52

2 tablespoons cold butter

Hash Brown Potatoes, page 162

Preheat oven to 350 degrees. Brush the pork tenderloins with the whole grain mustard. Wrap the prosciutto ham around the pork tenderloins, covering as much as possible. Use toothpicks to hold ham to the pork if necessary. Season the pork with salt and pepper. Heat the Clarified Butter in a medium sauté pan. When hot, sear the pork until golden brown on all sides. Transfer pork to the oven to finish cooking, about 15-18 minutes for medium. Remove pork from the pan and allow to rest for 10 minutes. Pour off almost all the grease. Return pan to the stove top and add the coffee and Beef Stock. Stir and scrape any browned bits off the bottom of the pan. Allow sauce to reduce by about 25%. Remove from heat and whisk in the cold butter, season with salt and freshly ground black pepper and keep warm. Carve the pork tenderloin on the bias into ½" slices. Spoon the Red Eye Gravy over the pork. Serve with the Hash Brown Potatoes.

Slow Roasted Prime Rib with au Jus

MAKES 8 SERVINGS

1 oven-ready rib roast

Olive oil

Steak Seasoning, page 180

3 tablespoons fresh rosemary, minced

1 pound carrot, celery, onion, cut in 2" pieces

1 cup water

1 cup red wine

Kosher salt

Black pepper

Creamed Horseradish, page 32

Preheat oven to 300 degrees. Rub the entire roast with olive oil, a very generous amount of Steak Seasoning and the chopped rosemary. Place the chopped vegetables in the bottom of a roasting pan and place the roast on top of the vegetables. Place a probe thermometer into the center of the roast and set for 115 degrees. Put the roast in the oven and turn the oven down to 200 degrees and roast until internal temperature is achieved. Remove the roast and turn oven up to 500 degrees. Allow the roast to rest until an internal temperature of 130 degrees is reached. Place the roast back into the preheated 500 degree oven for about 10 minutes or until you've achieved your desired crust. Remove and transfer roast to a cutting board and cover with foil for at least 30 minutes until serving. Strain out the juices from the roasting pan, reserve and place the pan over low heat and deglaze with the water. Add the wine and reduce by half. Remove the grease from the roasting juices and add to the sauce. Season with salt and pepper and serve on the side with the Creamed Horseradish.

Slow Roasted Prime Rib with au Jus page 124

Steak au Poivre

MAKES 4 SERVINGS

4 12-ounce prime New York strip steaks

⅓ cup whole peppercorns

Kosher salt

3 tablespoons Clarified Butter, page 172

¾ cup cognac

2 cups heavy cream

1 cup Burgundy Wine Sauce, page 28

2 teaspoons fresh chives, minced

Preheat oven to 375 degrees. Put the peppercorns into a plastic bag and, using either a rolling pin or meat mallet, crush the peppercorns into large pieces. Place peppercorns in a pie pan and season with a large pinch of salt. Press the steaks firmly into the peppercorns, fully coating both sides. Heat a large sauté pan over medium high heat. Add the butter and, working in batches if needed, sear the steaks until well browned on both sides, about 3 minutes per side. Transfer steaks to a baking tray and put in the oven to finish cooking. Drain excess grease from the sauté pan and deglaze with the cognac then add the heavy cream and the wine sauce. Bring sauce to a simmer and cook until reduced by about half. Season with salt and set aside. Remove steaks from the oven, 10-12 minutes for medium rare and put steaks on four individual plates. Spoon the sauce evenly over each steak and top with the minced chives.

Steak Diane

MAKES 4 SERVINGS

8 4-ounce prime filet mignons

Steak Seasoning, page 180

4 tablespoons Clarified Butter, page 172

2 cups button mushrooms, sliced

¼ cup cognac

1¼ cups Steak Diane Sauce, page 46

2 teaspoons fresh parsley, chopped

Kosher salt

Black pepper

Toasted Barley Risotto, page 168

Preheat oven to 375 degrees. Season filets with Steak Seasoning and set aside. Heat the butter in a large sauté pan until hot. Add the filets and sear until golden brown on both sides. Transfer sauté pan to the oven to finish cooking until desired temperature, about 10 minutes for medium rare. Remove pan from the oven. Remove filets from the pan and put on a serving platter. Add the sliced mushrooms to the pan and cook until they start to brown, about 7-8 minutes over medium high. Deglaze pan with the cognac. Add the Diane sauce and bring to a simmer. Turn off heat and season with salt and pepper. Fold in the chopped parsley and spoon sauce over the filets. Serve with the Toasted Barley Risotto on the side.

Stilton Stuffed Filet

MAKES 4 SERVINGS

4 8-ounce prime filet mignons

6 tablespoons Stilton cheese, crumbled

8 slices bacon

4 metal skewers

Steak Seasoning, page 180

3 tablespoons Merlot Butter, page 174

Eddie's Potatoes, page 160

Preheat grill to high. Using a paring knife cut a one and a half inch pocket into the side of each filet. Stuff each filet with 1½ tablespoons of the Stilton cheese. Using your finger, pinch the hole closed. Wrap two slices of bacon around each stuffed filet and skewer with a metal skewer to hold the bacon in place. Season the filet with Steak Seasoning and grill to desired temperature, about 6 minutes per side for medium rare. Place filets on a serving platter and remove skewers. Brush liberally with the Merlot Butter and serve with the Eddie's Potatoes.

There is nothing better than a filet grilled to perfection paired with a creamy and pungent Stilton bleu cheese, smoky bacon and smothered in a rich merlot wine enhanced butter.

Stilton Stuffed Filet page 126

Tournedos Rossini

MAKES 4 SERVINGS

8 1½-ounce foie gras medallions

Steak Seasoning, page 180

Brioche Bread, cut into 8 3" rounds

8 4-ounce prime filet mignons

2 tablespoons Clarified Butter, page 172

1 cup Truffled Madeira Sauce, page 50

Preheat oven to 375 degrees. Heat a large, dry sauté pan over medium heat. Season foie gras medallions with Steak Seasoning and sear in the dry skillet until crusted and golden brown on both sides, about 2 minutes per side. Remove foie gras from the pan and place on a cooling rack, reserving the grease. Working in batches if necessary, lightly toast the brioche discs in the reserved grease until golden brown. Place two toasted brioche croutons on each of four dinner plates. Season the filets with the steak seasoning. Add the Clarified Butter to the sauté pan and heat over medium high heat. Sear filets until golden brown, flip and transfer pan with the filets to the oven to finish cooking, about 10 minutes for medium rare. Remove pan from oven and place a filet on top of each brioche toast. Add the foie gras to the skillet and gently reheat. Place a foie gras medallion on top of each filet. Add the Truffled Madeira Sauce to the pan and heat until hot. Spoon some sauce over each filet and serve with any leftover sauce on the side.

Tuscan Strip Steak

MAKES 4 SERVINGS

4 12-ounce prime New York strip steaks

3 tablespoons olive oil

Steak Seasoning, page 180

4 tablespoons Tapenade Butter, page 176

Tuscan Tomato-Olive Relish

Toss the New York strip steaks with the olive oil and season liberally with the Steak Seasoning. Preheat grill to high. Grill steaks to desired temperature, about 6-7 minutes per side for medium rare. Place steaks on a serving platter and brush with the Tapenade Butter and top each steak with a generous portion of the relish.

Tuscan Tomato-Olive Relish

2 cups grape tomato, split in half

2 tablespoons red onion, minced

2 teaspoons garlic, minced

5 tablespoons fresh basil, chopped

3 tablespoons extra virgin olive oil

1 tablespoon balsamic vinegar

1 teaspoon fresh lemon zest

¾ cup assorted olives, pitted and chopped

½ teaspoon crushed red pepper

Kosher salt

Black pepper

Sugar (optional)

In a small mixing bowl, gently toss all ingredients together. Taste and season with salt and pepper. Add a touch of sugar to help bring out the flavor of the tomatoes, if needed.

Wagyu Flat Iron Steak

MAKES 4 SERVINGS

4 8-ounce Wagyu flat iron steaks

1 tablespoon olive oil

2 tablespoons Brown Sugar BBQ Rub, page 178

¾ cup Smoked Red Chili Chimichurri Sauce, page 42

¾ cup Pico de Gallo

Crispy Fried Onions, page 100

1 tablespoon fresh cilantro, chopped

Rub flat iron steak with the olive oil and coat with the Barbecue Rub and set aside for 30 minutes. Preheat grill to high. Grill flat iron steaks over the hottest part of your grill for about 3 minutes per side for medium rare. Remove from the grill and allow to rest for 10 minutes before slicing against the grain into ¼ inch slices. Spoon the chimichurri sauce over the steak slices and top with the Pico de Gallo, fried onions and chopped cilantro.

Pico de Gallo

1 cup fresh tomato, diced

2 tablespoons red onion, minced

1 tablespoon jalapeño, minced

2 teaspoons fresh cilantro, chopped

1 tablespoon extra virgin olive oil

1 tablespoon fresh lime juice

1 teaspoon garlic, minced

Kosher salt

Black pepper

Gently toss all ingredients in a small bowl and mix well until combined. Season with salt and pepper and allow to sit at room temperature for 20 minutes before serving.

Wagyu Flat Iron Steak page 128

Andouille Sausage and Shrimp Stuffed Quail

MAKES 4 SERVINGS

8 5-ounce semi-boneless quail

2 cups Andouille Sausage and Shrimp Stuffing

2 tablespoons olive oil

1 tablespoon Blackened Spice, page 178

1½ cups Andouille Sausage Gravy, page 26

Creamed Corn, page 160

Preheat oven to 400 degrees. Wash out the cavity of each quail and pat dry with paper towels. Stuff each quail with four tablespoons of the sausage and shrimp stuffing. Rub the quail with the olive oil and liberally coat each one with the Blackened Spice. Place the quail in a baking dish and place in the oven for 35-40 minutes or until the stuffing reaches 155 degrees. Remove from the oven and pour the sausage gravy over the quail. Serve 2 quail per person with the Creamed Corn.

Andouille Sausage and Shrimp Stuffing

MAKES 2 CUPS

2 sticks butter

¼ pound andouille sausage, ¼" diced

¼ cup yellow onion, diced

¼ cup celery, diced

¼ cup green pepper, diced

1 tablespoon garlic, minced

½ pound shrimp, roughly chopped

1 tablespoon Blackened Spice, page 178

4 eggs, lightly beaten

1½ cups Panko bread crumbs

Kosher salt

Black pepper

Melt the butter in a large sauté pan over medium heat. Increase heat to medium high and add the sausage and continue to cook until well browned, about 5-6 minutes. Add the onions, celery and green pepper, turn heat down to medium low and continue to cook until vegetables are soft, about 10-12 minutes. Add the garlic, shrimp and Blackened Spice and continue to cook until the shrimp are fully cooked. Remove from heat and transfer to a mixing bowl. Allow stuffing to cool to room temperature and fold in the eggs and the bread crumbs. Season with salt and pepper and refrigerate until needed.

Barbecue Spiced Duck Breasts

MAKES 4 SERVINGS

4 12-ounce duck breasts, skin scored in checker board pattern

4 teaspoons Brown Sugar BBQ Rub, page 176

12 Corn and Duck Confit Ravioli, page 132

1 cup Sweet Potato Gravy with Grand Marnier, page 48

Preheat oven to 350 degrees. Liberally season the duck breasts with the barbecue spice and place into a cold sauté pan. Saute, skin side down over medium low heat until skin is crispy and most of the fat is rendered, about 20-25 minutes. Turn up heat to medium high. Flip duck and transfer to the oven to finish cooking, about 8 minutes for medium. Cook the ravioli in simmering water for 3-4 minutes. Drain and place on 4 warmed dinner plates. Slice the duck on the bias in ¼" thick slices and fan across the top of the ravioli. Spoon the sweet potato gravy over the ravioli and around the duck. Continued on page 132.

Barbecue Spiced Duck Breasts page 130

Barbecue Spiced Duck Breasts

CONTINUED

Corn and Duck Confit Ravioli

¾ cup Creamed Corn, chilled, page 160

½ pound duck confit meat, shredded

¼ wheel Boursin cheese

1 teaspoon parsley, chopped

¼ teaspoon kosher salt

¼ teaspoon white pepper

12 wonton skins

1 egg, beaten with 1 tablespoon of water

In a small mixing bowl, mix the Creamed Corn with the duck confit, Boursin, chopped parsley and salt and pepper. Place the wonton skins on a flat surface and brush the edges with the egg wash. Spoon one ounce of the filling onto the center of each square. Fold each square in half, creating a triangle, making sure to push all excess air out and that the edges are fully sealed. Place the ravioli on a cookie sheet lined with parchment paper and cover with a damp cloth until needed.

Mustard Dressing

¼ cup red wine vinega
2 teaspoons Dijon mustard
2 teaspoons whole grain mustard
1 tablespoon shallots, minced
1 green onion, chopped
1 cup extra virgin olive oil
Kosher salt
Black pepper

Place vinegar, mustards, shallot and onion in a food processor and puree on high. With motor running, slowly drizzle in olive oil. Season with salt and pepper. Store leftovers for 5 days.

Grilled BBQ Chicken with Black-eyed Pea Relish

MAKES 4 SERVINGS

4 8-ounce boneless chicken breasts, skin on

1 tablespoon olive oil

2 teaspoons Brown Sugar BBQ Rub, page 178

¼ cup Southern Comfort Peach Barbecue Sauce, page 44

2 cups Black-eyed Pea and Corn Relish

4 lime wedges

Coat the chicken in the olive oil and the barbecue rub and allow to marinate for 2-3 hours in the refrigerator. Preheat grill to high and grill the chicken until nice char marks have formed. Flip chicken, brush with the barbecue sauce and continue to cook while basting until cooked through, about 10 minutes. Remove from grill and serve with the Black-eyed Pea and Corn Relish, lime wedges and barbecue sauce on the side.

Black-eyed Pea and Corn Relish

1½ cups black-eyed peas, cooked

¼ cup yellow onion, minced

¼ cup red onion, minced

¼ cup red pepper, diced

1 tablespoon jalapeño, minced

1 teaspoon garlic, minced

2 ears fresh cut corn kernels, cooked

¼ cup Mustard Dressing

Kosher salt

Black pepper

Toss all ingredients together until well mixed. Allow to sit for 30 minutes to let flavors develop.

Meyer Lemon Chicken

MAKES 4 SERVINGS

4 8-ounce boneless chicken breasts, skin on

Kosher salt and black pepper

1 cup flour

6 tablespoons Clarified Butter, page 172

2 cups fingerling potatoes, roasted until tender and cut in half

1 cup fresh asparagus, cut into 1" pieces

¾ cup Meyer Lemon Vinaigrette, page 134

1 tablespoon fresh chives, chopped

4 lemon wedges

Preheat oven to 375 degrees. Season chicken breasts liberally with salt and pepper and dredge in the flour to thoroughly coat. In a large sauté pan, over medium high, heat 4 tablespoons of the butter until hot and add the chicken breasts, skin side down, and cook until skin is golden brown and crispy, about 4-5 minutes. Flip chicken and place pan in the oven to finish cooking, about 10-12 minutes. While chicken is cooking, heat another sauté pan with the remaining butter over medium high heat. Add the fingerling potatoes and the asparagus pieces, reduce heat to medium and continue to cook, stirring frequently until potatoes are hot and asparagus is tender. Place mixture on a serving platter. Remove chicken from the oven and place on top of the potato/asparagus mixture. Drain any grease from the pan the chicken was in and, off the heat, add the Meyer Lemon Vinaigrette and swirl to gently warm. Pour the sauce over the chicken and top with the chopped chives. Serve with the lemon wedges.

Meyer Lemon Chicken page 132

Meyer Lemon Vinaigrette

MAKES 1¼ CUPS

3 Meyer lemons, juiced and zested

2 teaspoons Dijon mustard

2 teaspoons rice vinegar

½ teaspoon fresh rosemary leaves, minced

1 small shallot, peeled and minced

1 cup extra virgin olive oil

1 tablespoon honey

Kosher salt

Black pepper

Using a food processor, puree the lemon juice and zest, Dijon mustard, rice vinegar, rosemary and shallot on high. With the motor running, slowly drizzle the olive oil in a thin and continuous stream. Add the honey and season with salt and pepper. Taste and add more honey if a sweeter taste is preferred.

Meyer lemons are a cross between a lemon and an orange. They have a sweeter less acidic taste than the common lemon. Here we add a splash of honey and some fresh rosemary to make a perfect complement to chicken. You can also use this as a glaze for grilled fish. Just brush it on at the last minute before taking off the grill. If you can't find Meyer lemons substitute ½ orange for 2 of the Meyer lemons in the recipe.

Pan Seared Duck with Shiitake Sticky Rice

MAKES 4 SERVINGS

4 8-ounce duck breasts, skin scored in checker board pattern

Kosher salt and black pepper

1 tablespoon sesame oil

1 cup red onion, julienned

1 cup carrots, julienned

4 heads baby bok choy, cleaned and chopped

1 teaspoon sesame seeds

½ cup fresh orange juice

¼ cup fresh lemon juice

¼ cup soy sauce

1 teaspoon fresh ginger, minced

2 tablespoons scallion, chopped

3 ounces Burgundy Wine Sauce, page 28

3 cups Shiitake Sticky Rice, page 166

Season duck breasts with salt and pepper. Place breasts, skin side down, in a cold sauté pan and place over medium low heat. Allow duck to render as much fat as possible and the skin is crispy and golden brown. It should take about 20-25 minutes. Turn temperature to high, flip duck and sear on the other side for 2 minutes. Remove duck from the pan and place on a cutting board. Drain off all but 2 tablespoons of the duck fat and keep pan on high heat. Add the sesame oil, onion, carrot and cook for 1 minute. Add the bok choy and cook just until wilted, about 2-3 minutes. Toss with the sesame seeds and season with salt and pepper. Divide the stir-fried vegetables among the four dinner plates. Return pan back to the stove over high and add the orange and lemon juices, soy sauce, ginger and chopped scallion. Reduce

Rosemary Mustard Glazed Chicken

MAKES 4 SERVINGS

4 8-ounce boneless, skinless chicken breasts

Kosher salt

Black pepper

3 tablespoons Clarified Butter, page 172

2 tablespoons Dijon mustard

1 tablespoon fresh rosemary, chopped

½ cup Gruyere cheese, grated

¼ cup bread crumbs

1 cup Burgundy Wine Sauce, page 28

Lyonnaise Potatoes, page 162

Preheat oven to 350 degrees. Season the chicken breasts with salt and pepper. Heat the butter in a large sauté pan over medium high heat. When hot, sear the chicken breasts in the butter until golden brown on one side. Flip chicken and turn heat down to medium and continue to cook for 2-3 more minutes. Turn off heat and brush chicken with the Dijon mustard. Sprinkle the rosemary over the chicken and divide the cheese over the chicken. Top each chicken breast evenly with the bread crumbs and transfer chicken to the oven to finish cooking, about 10 minutes. Serve chicken with the wine sauce and Lyonnaise Potatoes on the side.

Pan Seared Duck with Shiitake Sticky Rice continued

liquid by half. Add the wine sauce and heat until hot. Season with salt and pepper. While sauce is reducing, slice the duck on the bias and evenly portion on top of the vegetables. Spoon the finished sauce over and around the duck and serve with the sticky rice.

Rosemary Mustard Glazed Chicken page 134

Sun-dried Tomato and Cheese Stuffed Chicken

MAKES 4 SERVINGS

4 8-ounce boneless, skinless, chicken breasts

½ cup Goat Cheese Stuffing (see box below)

Kosher salt

Black pepper

1 cup flour

3 tablespoons Clarified Butter, page 172

½ cup white wine

1 fresh lemon, juiced

4 tablespoons Steak Butter, cold, page 176

3 tablespoons sun-dried tomato, julienned

2 tablespoons basil pesto

Preheat oven to 350 degrees. Cut a 1x2" pocket in the side of each chicken breast. Stuff each breast with 2 tablespoons of the stuffing. Season chicken with salt and pepper and dredge in the flour, fully coating both sides. In a large skillet over medium high heat, sear the chicken in the butter until golden brown. Flip chicken and transfer to the oven to finish cooking and stuffing is hot, about 15 minutes. Remove pan from the oven, drain excess grease, and place chicken breasts on a serving platter. Deglaze pan with the white wine and lemon juice and allow sauce to reduce by half. Turn off heat and whisk in the cold Steak Butter a little at a time until fully incorporated and creamy. Stir in the sun-dried tomatoes and season with salt and pepper. Spoon the sauce over the chicken and spoon the pesto around the chicken.

Voodoo Jerked Chicken

MAKES 4 SERVINGS

1 5-pound whole chicken

2 tablespoons olive oil

Caribbean Jerk Spice, page 178

1 lemon, cut in half

2 fresh rosemary sprigs

2 cinnamon sticks

1 plantain, peeled and cut into 1" chunks

Oil for frying

1 cup Vanilla Bean Butter Sauce, page 50

4 cups Honey and Rum Black Beans

Preheat oven to 425 degrees. Rub chicken inside and out with the olive oil and liberally coat the entire chicken with the Jerk Spice. Place chicken on a roasting rack in a roasting pan and stuff the chicken cavity with the lemon halves, rosemary sprig and cinnamon sticks. Roast chicken in the oven for 30 minutes. Turn heat down to 375 degrees and continue to roast until a thermometer inserted into the joint between the thigh and the leg registers 165 degrees. Remove from oven and loosely cover in foil and allow to rest for 20 minutes. While the chicken is resting, heat oil to 300 degrees and deep fry the plantain chunks until soft and just beginning to color, about 3 minutes. Remove plantains and place each chunk between 2 pieces of wax paper and, using a heavy mallet, smash each chunk into a flat disc. Heat oil to 375 degrees and fry plantain disc until golden brown and crispy, about 2-3 minutes. Drain on paper towels and season with salt and pepper. Serve chicken with the plantains, Vanilla Bean Butter Sauce and the Honey and Rum Black Beans.

Voodoo Jerked Chicken

CONTINUED

Honey and Rum Black Beans

1 red pepper, diced

1 jalapeño, minced

1 small red onion, diced

2 tablespoons olive oil

⅔ cup dark rum

4 cups black beans, cooked

⅓ cup honey

4 tablespoons fresh cilantro, chopped

4 tablespoons green onion, chopped

Kosher salt

Black pepper

In a large sauté pan, sauté red pepper, jalapeño and red onion in olive oil just until soft, about 2 minutes. Add the rum and reduce by 25%. Remove from heat and pour into a mixing bowl. Allow mixture to cool to room temperature and then fold in the rest of the ingredients. Season with salt and pepper.

Goat Cheese Stuffing

½ pound goat cheese, softened
4 tablespoons sun-dried tomato, julienned
1 tablespoon basil pesto
2 teaspoons fresh lemon juice
¼ teaspoon crushed red pepper
¼ teaspoon sugar
Kosher salt
Black pepper

Whip the goat cheese until soft, about 2-3 minutes. Add the rest of the ingredients, season with salt and pepper and mix thoroughly. Place stuffing in a pastry bag and use to stuff chicken breasts or pork chops.

Voodoo Jerked Chicken page 136

Barbecue Glazed
Cedar Plank Salmon

MAKES 4 SERVINGS

4 8-ounce fresh salmon fillets

4 5x7 inch cedar cooking planks

½ cup Seafood Barbecue Sauce,
page 42

1 pound asparagus, trimmed of any
woody parts

2 teaspoon olive oil

Kosher salt

Black pepper

Lemon Roasted Garlic Aioli, page 38

Soak the cedar planks in water for 2
hours. Preheat grill to high. Add
the cedar planks to the grill until
they start to smoke, about 4
minutes. Flip the planks, turn heat
down to medium and add a salmon
fillet to the top of each plank.
Brush each fillet with the barbecue
sauce, cover the grill and cook until
done, about 12 minutes. Check
salmon often, if wood catches on
fire use a spray bottle of water to
put out the flames and turn the heat
down. During the last few minutes
of cooking, toss the asparagus with
the olive oil and season with salt
and pepper and place on the grill
until nicely charred and asparagus
is soft. Serve the salmon with the
Lemon Roasted Garlic Aioli and the
grilled asparagus.

Blackened Scallops
with Bleu Cheese Sauce

MAKES 4 SERVINGS

20 fresh U-10 sized scallops

3 tablespoons Blackened Spice,
page 178

4 tablespoons Clarified Butter,
page 172

1 tablespoon olive oil

12-ounces fresh green beans,
blanched

4 tablespoons Caramelized Red
Onion Jam, page 30

Kosher salt

Black pepper

1 cup Bleu Cheese Sauce, page 48

4 fresh lemon wedges

2 teaspoons fresh chives, minced

Liberally coat the scallops with the
Blackened Spice. In a large cast
iron skillet, heat the butter over high
heat, just until it starts to smoke.
Carefully add the scallops and cook
until a dark brown, about 2-3
minutes. Flip scallops and cook
until barely cooked through, another
2-3 minutes. Remove from skillet
and place on a draining rack. In a
large sauté pan heat the olive oil
over medium heat. Add the green
beans and the onion jam, season
with salt and pepper and toss until
hot. Portion 4 tablespoons of the
bleu cheese sauce on the bottom of
four dinner plates. Divide the green
bean mixture evenly between the
dinner plates. Place 5 scallops on
top of the green beans. Garnish
with the lemon wedges and minced
chives.

Black Truffle
and Lobster Risotto

MAKES 6-8 SERVINGS

8 cups Lobster Stock, page 52

4 tablespoons truffle juice, from
canned truffles

4 ounces butter

½ cup onion, minced

3 cups Arborio rice

1 cup Madeira wine

½ cup Parmesan cheese, shredded

½ cup heavy cream

1½ teaspoon kosher salt

2 ounces canned truffle slices

1 pound lobster meat, cooked and
chopped

1 tablespoon truffle oil

2 teaspoons fresh chives, minced

Combine the Lobster Stock and the
truffle juice in a small stock pot and
bring to a low simmer. In a heavy
bottomed sauce pan, sweat the
onions in the butter over
medium/low heat until soft, but not
colored, about 8-9 minutes. Add
the Arborio and stir constantly until
the rice is lightly toasted, about 3-4
minutes. Increase heat to medium,
add the Madeira wine and stir until
completely absorbed. Add the
simmering stock in one cup
additions, stirring constantly. Wait
until each addition is almost
completely absorbed before adding
the next one cup of stock. When all
the stock is completely absorbed,
taste to see if rice is tender, but still
firm to the touch. If needed, add
more boiling water in ½ cup
increments until desired texture is
achieved. Turn off heat; fold in
Parmesan cheese, heavy cream,
salt, truffles and lobster. Taste and
adjust seasonings. Place a lid on
the risotto and allow to sit on the
counter for 10 minutes. If risotto is
too thick, thin with some hot stock.

Black Truffle and Lobster
Risotto continued

It should be very creamy, not heavy and
sticky. Spoon risotto into a serving bowl
and drizzle the top with the truffle oil,
a little Parmesan cheese and minced
chives. Serve immediately.

Blackened Scallops with Bleu Cheese Sauce page 138

Eddie's Crab and Bleu Cheese Stuffed Shrimp

MAKES 4 SERVINGS

16 large 8-12 count shrimp

1 cup Pan Fried Crab Cake Mixture, page 72

1 cup Bacon and Gorgonzola Cheese Crust, page 26

½ cup Panko bread crumbs

¼ cup Clarified Butter, page 172

¼ cup white wine

Preheat oven to 400 degrees. De-shell shrimp and clean, leaving the tails on. Butterfly the shrimp through the back so they sit flat on a work surface. Place 1 tablespoon of Crab Cake Mixture on top of each shrimp and gently flatten. Add one tablespoon of the bleu cheese crust to the top of each shrimp and also gently flatten. Place the shrimp into a baking dish or casserole dish and evenly top the shrimp with the bread crumbs. Spoon the butter and the white wine over the shrimp and bake in the oven for 20 minutes until the tops are golden brown and the shrimp is cooked through.

Large shrimp topped with a delicious crab mixture and finished with our signature bleu cheese and bacon crust makes this a classic Eddie Merlots dish and is also our longest running seafood entrée.

Fresh Horseradish and Herb Crusted Walleye

MAKES 4 SERVINGS

4 7-ounce walleye fillets

1 cup flour

1 cup egg wash

4 cups Fresh Horseradish and Herb Crust

½ cup Clarified Butter, page 172

1 cup A Really Good Tartare Sauce, page 26

Fresh lemon wedges

Brussels Sprouts, page 158

Rinse and pat dry the walleye fillets. (Have your butcher remove the skin and bones). Dredge the fillets in the flour and shake off any excess. Dip the fillets in the egg wash and dredge in the horseradish crust, fully coating both sides, set aside. In a large sauté pan, heat the butter over medium heat, add the breaded walleye fillets and pan fry until golden brown, about 5-6 minutes. Flip fillets, reduce heat slightly and continue to cook until golden brown and cooked through. Drain fillets on a cooling rack and serve with the tartare sauce, lemon wedges and the Brussels Sprouts.

Fresh Horseradish and Herb Crust

2 cups Panko bread crumbs

2 cups fresh horseradish, grated

1 tablespoon fresh parsley, chopped

1 tablespoon fresh chives, chopped

1 teaspoon fresh rosemary, chopped

2 teaspoons kosher salt

2 teaspoons black pepper

Combine all ingredients together and mix thoroughly.

Grilled Ahi Tuna Steaks with Spicy Mustard Sauce

MAKES 4 SERVINGS

4 8-ounce ahi tuna steaks

3 tablespoons soy sauce

1 teaspoon Dijon mustard

2 teaspoons sesame oil

2 tablespoons water

1 fresh lime, juiced

4 tablespoons green onions, sliced

Kosher salt

Black pepper

1 cup Spicy Asian Style Mustard Sauce, page 44

Tempura Green Beans, page 74

In a small mixing bowl, whisk together the soy sauce, mustard, sesame oil, water, lime juice, green onions and salt and pepper. Reserve half of the liquid. Place the tuna steaks and the other half of the liquid in a sealable plastic bag and marinate in the refrigerator for 2 hours. Preheat grill to as high as it goes. Remove tuna from the marinade and discard used marinade. Grill tuna for 1 minute on each side, keeping as rare as possible. Slice tuna on the biased in ½" slices. Spoon the reserved marinade over the tuna and serve with the Spicy Asian Style Mustard Sauce for dipping and the Tempura Green Beans.

Eddie's Crab and Bleu Cheese Stuffed Shrimp page 140

Lobster Ravioli with Duck Confit

MAKES 4-6 SERVINGS

½ cup leeks, sliced

½ ounce Clarified Butter, page 172

1 cup duck confit, rough chopped

1 cup butternut squash, diced and cooked until fork tender

1 cup heavy cream

1 cup mascarpone cheese

2 tablespoons Steak Butter, page 176

Kosher salt

Black pepper

25 lobster ravioli

10 fresh sage leaves

½ cup Parmesan cheese, shredded

Bring a large pot of salted water to a boil. In a medium sauté pan, over medium heat, sauté the leeks in the butter until very soft, about 8-10 minutes, stirring often. Add the duck confit and the butternut squash and continue to cook until mixture starts to brown, about 7-8 minutes. Add the heavy cream and bring to a boil. Allow cream to reduce by about half, whisk in the mascarpone cheese. Turn off heat and whisk in the Steak Butter and the sage leaves. Continue to whisk until sauce is smooth and creamy. Season with salt and pepper and keep warm. Cook the ravioli in salted boiling water for 5 minutes. Drain ravioli and portion into pasta bowls. Spoon the sauce over the ravioli and top with the shredded Parmesan cheese.

Lobster Stuffing for Ravioli

MAKES 25

3 slices Texas Toast bread, crust removed

½ cup 2% milk

2 large shallots, minced

4 tablespoons duck fat or Clarified Butter, page 172

1 cup heavy cream

¾ pound lobster meat, cooked and roughly chopped

2 tablespoons fresh herbs, chopped

Kosher salt

Black pepper

25 wonton skins

1 egg, lightly beaten

Cut bread into 1" cubes and place in a small mixing bowl. Pour milk over the bread and allow to soak for ½ hour. In a small sauté pan, over medium heat, cook the shallots in duck fat or butter until soft, about 4-5 minutes. Add the heavy cream and reduce by half. Remove cream mixture from heat and allow to cool to room temperature. Once cool, fold in lobster meat. Using your hands, squeeze all the milk from the bread cubes and place soggy bread back into the mixing bowl. Add the lobster cream mixture, chopped fresh herbs, season with salt and pepper and toss until well mixed. Refrigerate mixture for 30 minutes to firm up. Place the wonton skins on a cutting board and brush the edges with the beaten egg. Place 1 tablespoon of the filling onto the center of each wonton skin. Fold the wontons over in half, creating a triangle. Gently squeeze out the air from the ravioli, making sure that both edges are sealed. Place finished ravioli on a cookie sheet, covered with a damp paper towel, in the refrigerator until ready to cook.

Maple and Apple Cider Glazed Sea Bass

MAKES 4 SERVINGS

4 8-ounce sea bass fillets

Kosher salt and black pepper

3 tablespoons Clarified Butter, page 172

1 pound fresh green beans, blanched

4 tablespoons Caramelized Red Onion Jam, page 30

4 tablespoons Maple-Apple Cider Vinaigrette, page 106

4 teaspoons Balsamic Syrup

Preheat oven to 375 degrees. Season the sea bass with salt and pepper. In a large sauté pan, heat 2 tablespoons butter over high heat and add the fish. Cook until golden brown, about 5 minutes. Flip and transfer fish to oven to finish cooking, about 15 minutes. Three minutes before sea bass is finished cooking, glaze each fillet with 1 tablespoon of the vinaigrette and allow to finish cooking. While fish is cooking, heat another sauté pan over medium heat, with the remaining 1 tablespoon of butter, until hot. Add the green beans and the red onion jam and cook until hot. Season with salt and pepper and divide mixture evenly among 4 dinner plates. Top each green bean mixture with a fillet and spoon 1 teaspoon of the balsamic syrup around each plate.

Balsamic Syrup

1 cup balsamic vinegar

¼ cup brown sugar

Combine the ingredients and place over medium high heat. Bring to a boil and reduce for 4 minutes. Carefully pour syrup into a 2 cup measuring cup. If volume is greater than ½ cup, continue to reduce. If volume is less than ½ cup, throw out and start over. Volume should be exactly ½ cup for the correct consistency at room temperature.

Maple and Apple Cider Glazed Sea Bass page 142

Minted Mango Salsa

MAKES 1½ CUPS

2 ripe mangos

2 ounces extra virgin olive oil

2 ounces rice vinegar

1 tablespoon brown sugar

2 tablespoons fresh mint leaves, chopped

3 tablespoons red pepper, diced

3 tablespoons green onion, sliced

2 tablespoons fresh cilantro, chopped

1 Serrano pepper, minced

Peel and seed mangos. Dice one mango into ½" pieces and place in a mixing bowl. Roughly chop the remaining mango and place in a food processor with the olive oil, rice vinegar, brown sugar and mint leaves. Process on high until smooth. Pour mango sauce into the bowl with diced mangos, add the rest of the ingredients, toss well and season with salt. Allow to sit for 30 minutes to allow flavors to develop before serving.

Mojito Fish Marinade

MAKES 2 CUPS

1½ tablespoons honey

6 pieces fresh sugar cane, cut into 3" lengths

½ cup water

½ cup sugar

1 cup rum

1 fresh lemon, juiced

½ teaspoon ground cinnamon

2 tablespoons fresh mint, rough chopped

1 teaspoon vanilla

In a small sauce pan, combine all ingredients. Bring mixture to a boil and reduce heat to a simmer, and cook for 5-6 minutes. Remove from heat and strain through a fine strainer. Refrigerate marinade until fully chilled before using.

Mojito Marinated Swordfish with Salsa

MAKES 4 SERVINGS

4 1"swordfish steaks, 8-ounces each

1 cup Mojito Fish Marinade

Kosher salt

Black pepper

1½ cups Minted Mango Salsa

Fresh lime wedges

Fresh cilantro sprigs

Marinate the steaks in the Mojito Fish Marinade for 2-3 hours. Preheat one side of the grill to high and the other side to medium. Remove the swordfish from the marinade and discard marinade. Pat fish dry with paper towels and lightly season with salt and pepper. Grill swordfish until nice grill marks are achieved on one side, about 5-6 minutes. Flip fish and move to the cooler side of the grill to finish cooking, being careful not to overcook. Pinkish swordfish is better tasting than well done. Place the fish steaks on a serving platter and top with the mango salsa. Garnish with the lime wedges and cilantro sprigs.

Mojito Marinated Swordfish with Mango Salsa page 144

Pan Fried Almond Crusted Walleye

MAKES 4 SERVINGS

4 8-ounce walleye fillets

1 cup flour

1 cup egg wash

3 cups Almond Breading

½ cup Clarified Butter, page 172

Kosher salt

Black pepper

Lemon wedges

A Really Good Tartare Sauce, page 26

Wash and pat dry the walleye fillets and set aside. Season flour and egg wash with a large pinch of salt and pepper. Dredge walleye in the flour and shake off excess. Next, dredge through the egg wash and crust with the Almond Breading, making sure to coat all sides. In a large sauté pan, heat butter over medium heat and add the breaded walleye fillets. Cook fillets until golden brown, about 8-9 minutes. Flip fish and lower heat slightly and continue to cook until golden brown and cooked through, about 8-9 more minutes. Transfer walleye to a cooling rack and season with salt and pepper while still hot. Serve with lemon wedges and tartare sauce.

Almond Breading

2 cups Panko bread crumbs
¾ + 1½ cups raw almonds, sliced
2 tablespoons fresh parsley, chopped
Kosher salt
Black pepper

Place bread crumbs and ¾ cup almonds in a food processor and pulse until fine. Transfer mixture to a small mixing bowl and fold in remaining 1½ cups sliced almonds and chopped parsley. Season with salt and pepper and mix thoroughly.

Pan Fried Soft Shell Crab

MAKES 4 SERVINGS

8 fresh soft shell crabs, large

1 cup corn meal

2 cups flour

2 eggs, lightly beaten

1 cup buttermilk

1 cup Clarified Butter, page 172

Kosher salt

Black pepper

½ cup Fresh Citrus and Smoked Chili Vinaigrette

Fresh parsley, chopped

Fresh lemon wedges

Wash and pat crabs dry with paper towels and set aside. Mix the corn meal and the flour with a heavy pinch of salt and set aside. Mix the eggs with the buttermilk and set aside. Dredge the crabs in the flour mixture and shake off excess. Dredge the crabs in the egg and buttermilk mixture, shake off excess and dredge once more in the flour and set aside. In a large sauté pan, over medium high heat, heat the butter until hot, carefully add the crabs and pan fry until golden brown, about 3 minutes. Flip and continue to cook for about 3-4 more minutes. Remove from pan and place on a cooling rack and sprinkle liberally with salt and pepper while still hot. Spoon the citrus and chili vinaigrette on a serving platter and top with the fried soft shell crabs. Garnish with the chopped parsley and lemon wedges.

Pan Fried Soft Shell Crab

CONTINUED

Fresh Citrus and Smoked Chili Vinaigrette

1 beef steak tomato, seeded and chopped

1 chipotle pepper (canned en adobo)

1 tablespoon sugar

1 orange, zested and juiced

1 lime, zested and juiced

1 lemon, zested and juiced

½ cup olive oil

Kosher salt

Black pepper

Puree the tomato, chipotle pepper, sugar, citrus juices and citrus zests in a food processor until smooth. With the motor still running, slowly drizzle the olive oil in a thin and continuous stream. Season with salt and pepper and allow to sit at room temperature for 30 minutes to allow flavors to develop. Stir well before using. Makes 1½ cups.

This vinaigrette goes well with all kinds of seafood. We have used it before on Grilled Snapper Tacos on a lunch menu and also with a grilled lobster salad with fingerling potatoes and green beans. The possibilities are only limited by your imagination.

Pan Fried Almond Crusted Walleye page 146

Sautéed Dover Sole

MAKES 1 SERVING

1 whole Dover sole (have your fish monger clean and prep for you)

¼ cup flour

Kosher salt

Black pepper

3 tablespoons Clarified Butter, page 172

4 tablespoons whole butter

1 tablespoon fresh lemon juice

2 tablespoons white wine

2 teaspoons fresh parsley, chopped

Preheat oven to 350 degrees. Season the flour liberally with salt and pepper. Lightly dredge the sole in the flour. Heat the Clarified Butter in a large sauté pan, over medium heat. Add the sole and sauté until golden brown on both sides, about 3-4 minutes per side. Transfer to the oven to finish cooking, about 14-16 minutes more. While fish is cooking, sauté the whole butter in a small sauté pan over medium heat until butter starts to brown. Add the fresh lemon juice, white wine, chopped parsley and salt and pepper and continue to cook until hot. Remove sole from oven, pat dry, de-bone and place on a serving platter. Pour the sauce over the sole and serve immediately.

> This dish is a staple on our annual holiday menu. It is presented and sauced tableside for a elegant and memorable presentation.

Sautéed Gulf Red Snapper with Rock Shrimp

MAKES 4 SERVINGS

4 7-ounce snapper fillets, skin on

Kosher salt

Black pepper

3 tablespoons Clarified Butter, page 172

6 ounces fresh rock shrimp

3 ounces white wine

4 ounces Lobster Butter, page 174

3 cups orzo pasta, cooked

3 cups fresh baby spinach leaf

¼ cup whole almonds, toasted

Fresh lemon wedges

Preheat oven to 375 degrees. Season the snapper fillets with salt and pepper. In a large sauté pan, heat the Clarified Butter over high heat. When hot, add the snapper, skin side down, and cook until golden brown, about 4-5 minutes. Flip snapper and transfer pan to the oven to finish cooking. When snapper is done, remove from the oven and place on a serving platter. Return sauté pan to the stove top over medium heat and add the rock shrimp and cook until pink. Deglaze with the white wine. Add the Lobster Butter, orzo pasta, spinach leaves and almonds and toss until hot. Season with salt and pepper and spoon mixture over the top of the snapper fillets. Serve with the lemon wedges.

Sautéed River Trout Meuniere

MAKES 2 SERVINGS

2 10-ounce fresh trout fillets

½ cup flour

Kosher salt

Black pepper

4 tablespoons Clarified Butter, page 172

½ cup white wine

1 fresh lemon, juiced

¼ cup capers

½ cup tomato, peeled, seeded and chopped

½ teaspoon fresh dill or parsley, chopped

½ cup cold Steak Butter, cut into 1" pieces, page 176

Fresh lemon wedges

Wash and pat dry the trout fillets with paper towels and set aside. Season the flour with a heavy pinch of salt and pepper. Heat the Clarified Butter in a large sauté pan, over medium high heat, until hot. Dredge the trout in the seasoned flour and sauté in the hot butter until golden brown, about 3 minutes. Flip fish, reduce heat to medium and continue to cook just until fish is cooked through, about 5-6 more minutes. Carefully transfer the trout to two serving plates. Drain grease from skillet and return back to the stove top. Deglaze with the white wine, lemon juice, capers, tomatoes and fresh dill. Cook until sauce is reduced by about 50%. Turn off the heat and whisk in the Steak Butter, whisking constantly until sauce is smooth and creamy. Season with salt and pepper. Spoon over the trout and serve with the lemon wedges.

Sautéed River Trout Meuniere page 148

Seafood Bouillabaisse

MAKES 4-6 SERVINGS

1 pound assorted raw fish heads, bones, tails, shrimp shells and lobster tail shells

3 whole bay leaves

Coarse sea salt

2 fresh thyme sprigs

1 small onion, quartered

1 tablespoon black peppercorns, whole

6 cups water

For the fish stock: Rinse the fish heads and place in a large soup pot with tails, bones, lobster shell, bay leaves, a generous pinch of sea salt, thyme sprigs, onion, black peppercorns and water. Place over high heat, cover, and bring to a boil. Decrease heat to a simmer and cook for 25 minutes. Strain through a fine strainer and discard solids. Set the stock aside.

¼ cup olive oil

1 cup onion, diced

½ cup fennel, diced

½ cup dry white wine

1 14½-ounce can tomatoes, diced

3 tablespoons fresh parsley, chopped

1 pinch saffron

8 ounces firm fish fillets, such as salmon or striped bass, skin and bones removed, cut into 1" pieces

8 ounces flaky fish fillets, such as black cod, halibut or sea bass, skin and bones removed, cut into 1" pieces

Seafood Bouillabaisse

CONTINUED

2 teaspoons garlic, crushed

4-5 drops Tabasco sauce

8 ounces mussels, cleaned and beards trimmed

1 large raw lobster tail, shell removed and used in the above stock recipe, meat cut into 1" pieces,

1 loaf bread, good and crusty

To make the stew: Place the olive oil in a large soup pot over medium heat. When hot, add the onion, fennel and a pinch of sea salt. Continue to cook until vegetables are soft, about 10 minutes, stirring frequently. Deglaze the pan with the wine and scrape any bits from the bottom of the pan. Add the reserved fish stock, tomatoes, parsley and saffron. Turn heat to high and bring to a boil. Reduce heat to a simmer and cook for 15 minutes. Increase the heat to high and add the fish, garlic and Tabasco sauce. Boil rapidly, uncovered, for 5-7 minutes, stirring occasionally. Remove the pot from the heat, add the mussels and lobster. Cover and let stand until the fish is cooked through and the mussels open, about 2-4 minutes. Discard any unopened mussels. Serve immediately with a good crusty bread to dunk in the broth.

Seared Ahi Tuna with Sesame Crust

MAKES 4 SERVINGS

4 8-ounce ahi tuna steaks

1 tablespoon white sesame seeds

1 tablespoon black sesame seeds

Kosher salt

Black pepper

2 tablespoons sesame oil

¾ cup Creamy Wasabi Sauce, page 32

1½ cups green seaweed salad

Pickled ginger

Soy sauce

Ginger-Garlic Dipping Sauce, page 36

Mix the sesame seeds with the salt and pepper. Press the tuna into the sesame seed mixture, making sure to coat all sides. In a large sauté pan, heat the sesame oil until hot and sear the tuna on all sides until the sesame seeds are lightly toasted, about 30 seconds per side. Place the finished tuna on a cutting board to rest. Spoon the Creamy Wasabi Sauce on the bottom of a serving platter. Place the seaweed salad in a strainer and allow to drain for a few minutes before placing on the serving platter. Thinly slice the tuna steaks on the biased and fan over the seaweed salad. Serve with the pickled ginger and Ginger-Garlic Dipping Sauce on the side.

Seared Ahi Tuna with Sesame Crust page 150

Steamed Mediterranean Halibut

MAKES 4 SERVINGS

4 8-ounce halibut fillets

2 tablespoons Clarified Butter, page 172

Kosher salt

Black pepper

4 cups Mediterranean Vegetable Broth, page 54

Extra virgin olive oil

½ cup Lemon and Roasted Garlic Aioli, page 38

Fresh chives, minced

1 loaf French style bread

In a large sauté pan with a tight fitting lid, heat the butter over medium high heat. Season halibut with salt and pepper and sear in the butter until golden brown on one side, about 5-6 minutes. Flip halibut and carefully add the Mediterranean Vegetable Broth, cover with the lid and reduce heat to a very low simmer. Cook until halibut flakes easily, about 12-15 minutes. Turn off heat and remove the lid and allow to cool for 10 minutes. Using a slotted spoon, gently place one halibut fillet into each of 4 bowls. Divide the broth evenly over the fish. Spoon the olive oil over the broth and divide the aioli over each piece of fish. Sprinkle each bowl with the minced chives and serve with the French bread on the side.

Sweet Ginger and Oolong Tea Marinated Cod

MAKES 4 SERVINGS

4 8-ounce fresh cod fillets

1 cup Sweet Ginger and Oolong Tea Marinade

3 tablespoons Clarified Butter, page 172

2 teaspoons sesame oil

1 cup carrots, julienned

1 cup red onion, julienned

1 cup shitake mushrooms, julienned

2 cups fresh green beans, trimmed and cut into 1" pieces

Kosher salt

Black pepper

¾ cup Ginger-Garlic Dipping Sauce, page 36

2 teaspoons sesame seeds

Place the cod fillets and the oolong tea marinade in a sealable plastic bag and refrigerate for at least 4 hours. Preheat oven to 400 degrees. Remove cod from the marinade, discarding used marinade, and pat fish dry with paper towels. Heat a large nonstick pan over medium high heat; add the butter and the cod fillets. Cook fish until golden brown on one side, about 4-5 minutes. Flip fish and transfer pan to the oven to finish cooking, about 10 minutes. While fish is in the oven, heat another medium sauté pan over high heat and when hot add the sesame oil, carrots, onion, mushrooms and green beans. Stir constantly until mushrooms are soft, about 5 minutes. Remove from heat and season with salt and pepper. Spoon the vegetables on a serving platter and top vegetables with the finished cod fillets. Spoon the Ginger-Garlic Dipping Sauce over the cod and sprinkle with sesame seeds.

Sweet Ginger and Oolong Tea Marinade

MAKES 2½ CUPS

2 cups water

2 tablespoons fresh ginger, minced

1 tablespoon garlic, minced

4 individual Oolong tea bags

¾ cup sweet soy sauce

2 tablespoons honey

Place the water, ginger and garlic in a small sauce pan and bring to a boil. Add the tea bags, remove from heat and allow to steep until mixture has cooled to room temperature. Remove the tea bags and whisk in the rest of the ingredients. Place marinade in the refrigerator until well chilled.

Oolong tea is a cross between black and green tea varieties; it has a full flavor and is packed with many health benefits. Here we use it as a base for a flavorful marinade that is enhanced with sweetened soy sauce and spicy fresh ginger. This also works well as a marinade for grilled or smoked chicken or duck.

Sweet Ginger and Oolong Tea Marinated Cod page 152

Lobster Mashed Potatoes

sides

Hash Brown Potatoes

Creamed Spinach Steak House Style

Grilled Baby Onions and Pickled Jalapeños

Asparagus and Potato "Risotto"

MAKES 4-6 SERVINGS

1 pound fresh asparagus

1 tablespoon Clarified Butter, page 172

1 tablespoon olive oil

2 shallots, minced

1 teaspoon garlic, minced

1½ pounds Idaho potatoes

½ cup white wine

3 cups Chicken Stock, page 52

Kosher salt

Black pepper

4 tablespoons Parmesan cheese, shredded

Cut off the woody ends of the asparagus and cut into ¼" pieces. Blanch asparagus and shock in ice water, drain and hold. Peel and cut the potatoes into ¼ inch dice. Sauté the shallots, garlic and potatoes in butter and olive oil for 5 minutes, or until shallots start to color. Add the white wine and simmer until dry. Add one cup of Chicken Stock and cook until most of the liquid is absorbed. Add another cup of stock and continue cooking until stock is absorbed. Add remaining Chicken Stock and cook until potatoes are tender. Season with salt and pepper. Fold in the Parmesan cheese and reserved asparagus.

Baked Macaroni and Cheese

MAKES 3-4 SERVINGS

1½ cups Five Cheese Sauce, page 36

4 cups cellentani pasta, cooked al dente

¼ cup Cheddar cheese, shredded

¼ cup Gruyere cheese, shredded

3 tablespoons bread crumbs, buttered

Over medium heat, warm the cheese sauce. Once warmed, add the pasta and toss until hot. Pour pasta into a casserole dish. Top with cheeses and bread crumbs. Bake at 375 degrees for 15 minutes or until golden brown.

We toyed around with adding a Macaroni and Cheese dish to our sides list for a couple of years. We wanted one that was rich, creamy and a little different, but still staying true to the classic feel. We developed a five cheese sauce with a handful of other ingredients and we haven't looked back since.

Bleu Cheese Cole Slaw

MAKES 8-10 SERVINGS

5 ounces green cabbage, ¼" shredded

5 ounces red cabbage, ¼" shredded

6 ounces carrots, ¼" shredded

¼ cup Pickled Red Onions, page 102

3 ounces bleu cheese crumbles

½ cup Steak House Bleu Cheese Dressing, page 108

¼ cup celery, ¼" chopped

1 teaspoon kosher salt

1 teaspoon black pepper

2 teaspoons sugar

Toss all the ingredients together until thoroughly mixed. Keep refrigerated.

This side dish was developed for our Burger Menu that we serve in the bar. Once again we challenged ourselves to give an upscale spin on a classic dish without taking away the feel of the perfect burger accompaniment.

Baked Macaroni and Cheese page 156

Bourbon-Jalapeño Creamed Corn

MAKES 4-6 SERVINGS

½ tablespoon Clarified Butter, page 172

1 large jalapeño, minced

2 cups fresh corn kernels

6 tablespoons Kentucky bourbon

5 cups Creamed Corn, page 160

2 tablespoons Kentucky bourbon

In a large saucepan, sauté the jalapeño in the butter just until soft. Add the fresh corn kernels and the 6 tablespoons of bourbon and continue to cook until liquid is reduced by about 50%. Mix in the Creamed Corn and 2 tablespoons bourbon. Stir until hot.

Brussels Spouts with Bacon and Parmesan

MAKES 4-6 SERVINGS

1½ pounds fresh Brussels sprouts

½ pound cippolini onions, quartered

4 slices of bacon, ½" dice

2 tablespoons Steak Butter, page 176

2 tablespoons Parmesan cheese, grated

Kosher salt

Black pepper

Trim the ends of the Brussels sprouts and cut in half. Blanch in boiling salted water 4-5 minutes or until tender. Drain and shock in ice water, pat dry. In a sauté pan, cook the bacon until crisp. Remove the bacon, reserving the bacon grease. Sauté the cipollini onions in the bacon grease until starting to brown. Add blanched Brussels sprouts; continue to cook until light golden brown. Remove from heat, fold in Steak Butter and reserved bacon. Season with salt and pepper. Top with Parmesan cheese.

Cipollini Onions and Charred Jalapeño

MAKES 3-4 SERVINGS

12 ounces cipollini onions

2 large jalapeños

4 tablespoons Clarified Butter, page 172

Kosher salt

Black pepper

Char the jalapeños over a gas flame until evenly charred. Chop jalapeños into 1" pieces and set aside. Sauté the cipollini onions in the Clarified Butter until soft and golden brown on both sides. Fold in the reserved charred jalapeños and season with salt and pepper.

You may have noticed that we use cipollini onions in quite a few of our recipes; the advantage to cipollini onions are that they are small and flat and the shape lends well to roasting. This combined with their sweetness and soft texture makes for a great addition to recipes where you might want to use whole caramelized onions. Cipollini onions are sweeter, having more residual sugar than garden-variety white or yellow onions, while not having the strong bite of other onions, and frankly they look really cool. However they can be a real pain to peel and sometimes may be a little hard to find, so they may not be quite the perfect onion, but they're probably as close as you can get.

Illini Onions and Charred Jalapeños page 158

Creamed Corn with Leeks

MAKES 4-6 SERVINGS

3 cups fresh corn kernels

¼ cup leeks, sliced

½ stick unsalted butter

1½ tablespoons sugar

1¼ teaspoons kosher salt

½ teaspoon white pepper

Pinch grated nutmeg

1½ cups heavy cream

1 12-ounce can creamed corn

Pinch cayenne pepper

In a large diameter sauce pan, melt butter over medium heat. Sauté the leeks until soft. Add fresh corn kernels, salt, white pepper and nutmeg. Cook for 10 minutes until sugar has thoroughly dissolved. Turn up heat to medium high and add heavy cream. Reduce cream by half, stirring often. Add canned cream corn, reduce heat to low and heat through for 15 minutes.

Creamed Spinach Steak House Style

MAKES 4-6 SERVINGS

1½ pounds frozen chopped spinach

¼ cup flour

1 stick butter

2 cups Half & Half

1½ teaspoons kosher salt

1 teaspoon white pepper

¼ teaspoon onion powder

Thaw the chopped spinach under running water. Squeeze out all excess water and set aside. In a heavy sauce pot, melt butter and whisk in the flour until smooth. Cook roux for 3-4 minutes, stirring constantly. Add seasonings and the Half & Half. Bring to a simmer, stirring often. Add squeezed spinach, mix well, lower heat and cook for 12-15 minutes.

Eddie's Garlic Mashed Potatoes

MAKES 6-8 SERVINGS

2½ pounds Idaho potatoes, peeled and cut in 1" cubes

1 stick unsalted butter, softened

2 tablespoons garlic cloves, roasted

2 teaspoons kosher salt

¼ teaspoon white pepper

1 cup Half & Half, warmed

Boil the potatoes until fork tender. Drain and return to pan. Add butter, roasted garlic and seasonings. Beat for 3 minutes until smooth. Slowly add warmed Half & Half, continue to beat for 3 more minutes. Serve immediately.

Eddie's Potatoes

MAKES 4-6 SERVINGS

1¼ pound potatoes, peeled and cut into ½" cubes

1½ tablespoons jalapeños, seeded and minced

1⅓ cups heavy cream

½ cup Gruyere cheese, shredded

⅓ cup Parmesan cheese, grated

1 teaspoon Tabasco sauce

1 cup Cheddar cheese, shredded

Kosher salt

Black pepper

Steam the potatoes for 30 minutes just until fork tender and not mushy. Put potatoes in a casserole dish.

Preheat oven to 375 degrees. In a sauce pan, bring the heavy cream and jalapeños to a simmer. Reduce by 25%, about 10-12 minutes. Whisk in the Gruyere, Parmesan cheese and Tabasco. Stir constantly until smooth. Season with salt and pepper. Pour over the potatoes, toss gently. Top potatoes with Cheddar cheese and bake for 15-18 minutes until hot and bubbly.

Creamed Spinach Steak House Style page 160

Hash Brown Casserole

MAKES 8-10 SERVINGS

3 pounds hash brown potatoes

4 tablespoons butter, melted

1½ cups Five Cheese Sauce, page 36

2 cups sour cream

½ cup green onions, sliced

2 cups Cheddar cheese, shredded

1½ teaspoon kosher salt

¾ teaspoon white pepper

Preheat oven to 350 degrees. Mix all ingredients together using ½ the amount of the Cheddar cheese. Pour into a buttered 9x13 pan. Cover the casserole evenly with the remaining Cheddar cheese. Cover with foil and bake for 45 minutes.

Hash Brown Potatoes

MAKES 4-6 SERVINGS

24 ounces frozen shredded potatoes

1 teaspoon kosher salt

½ teaspoon white pepper

¾ cup Clarified Butter, page 172

1 teaspoon fresh chives, chopped

Thaw potatoes in refrigerator overnight. Mix thawed potatoes with salt and pepper. Place the Clarified Butter into an 8-inch nonstick sauté pan. Add potato mixture and pat down firmly. Place entire skillet in the refrigerator for 1-2 hours to firm. Put skillet over medium heat; cook for 6-7 minutes. Do not stir. Place a pie pan or dinner plate on top of the skillet and flip pan so potatoes end up on the plate. Return potatoes to skillet, brown side up. Reshape if necessary and place back on burner. Cook for an additional 6-7 minutes until golden brown. Slide out of skillet onto serving dish. Garnish with chopped chives.

Lobster Mashed Potatoes

MAKES 4-6 SERVINGS

4 cups Eddie's Garlic Mashed Potatoes, page 160

½ cup lobster meat, cooked and chopped

4 tablespoons Lobster Butter, page 174

2 teaspoons fresh chives, chopped

Sauté the lobster meat in the Lobster Butter until warm. Pour the lobster mixture over the mashed potatoes. Top with the chopped chives.

Lyonnaise Potatoes

MAKES 3-4 SERVINGS

1 pound Idaho potatoes

1 cup white onion, sliced

4 tablespoons Clarified Butter, page 172

Fresh parsley, chopped

Steam or bake potatoes until soft. Peel potatoes after cooled to room temperature. Slice potatoes into ¼" slices and cook in the butter until brown. Add onion and season with salt and pepper to taste. Cook until onions are soft. Garnish with chopped parsley.

Hash Brown Potatoes page 162

Potato Croquettes

MAKES 4-6 SERVINGS

2 cups leftover mashed potatoes

¼ cup red pepper, small diced

2 tablespoons green onion, chopped

3-4 drops Tabasco sauce

¼ cup flour

3 eggs, beaten

½ cup buttermilk

2 cups Panko bread crumbs

2 teaspoons kosher salt

1 teaspoon black pepper

Thoroughly mix the mashed potatoes with the Tabasco, red pepper and green onion. Portion into eight patties and refrigerate for one hour. Mix eggs and buttermilk. Season the bread crumbs with salt and pepper. Dredge the patties in flour, then egg mixture and finally the bread crumbs. Pan fry the croquettes in Clarified Butter until hot in the middle and golden brown on both sides. Drain on cooling rack and keep warm until ready to serve.

Roasted Mushrooms

MAKES 4-6 SERVINGS

5 pounds assorted exotic mushrooms such as portobello, shiitake, cremini or oyster

3 tablespoons garlic, chopped

⅓ cup fresh parsley, chopped

½ cup olive oil

2½ teaspoons kosher salt

2½ teaspoons black pepper

½ teaspoon crushed red pepper

Clean any excess dirt from the mushrooms, do not rinse. Cut mushrooms into large bite-size pieces. In a large mixing bowl toss with the rest of the ingredients. Preheat oven to 500 degrees. Spread mushrooms evenly on 2 cookie sheets. Roast mushrooms for 10 minutes. Using a metal spatula, stir mushrooms, scraping any bits stuck to the sheet pans. Continue to roast for 10 more minutes. Repeat stirring process. Continue cooking and stirring until mushrooms are dry with no liquid on pans and are evenly browned.

Rosemary Cheese Polenta

MAKES 12 CAKES

1 stick butter

1 small shallot, minced

6 cups Chicken Stock, page 52

1 tablespoon garlic, roasted

2 teaspoons kosher salt

1½ teaspoons dry mustard

¾ teaspoon black pepper

¼ teaspoon turmeric

¾ pound corn meal

½ cup Gruyere cheese

¼ cup Parmesan cheese

2 egg yolks

1½ teaspoon fresh rosemary, minced

In a medium sauce pan, sauté the shallot in the butter until soft. Add the Chicken Stock, roasted garlic, salt, dry mustard, pepper and turmeric. Slowly whisk in the corn meal, stirring until smooth. Reduce heat to low and cook for 15 minutes, stirring often. Remove from heat and stir in cheese, egg yolks and rosemary. Pour into a nonstick baking pan. Place in refrigerator until firm. Once firm, cut into desired shapes. Pan fry in butter until golden brown and crispy on both sides.

Roasted Mushrooms page 164

Shiitake Sticky Rice

1½ tablespoons sesame oil

½ cup onion, minced

1 cup shiitake mushrooms, julienned

¼ cup Chinese sausage

4 tablespoons white wine

1½ cups sticky rice

2 tablespoons soy sauce

1½ cups Chicken Stock, page 52

1½ tablespoons fresh cilantro, chopped

In a saucepan, sauté the onion in the sesame oil over medium heat until soft, about 5 minutes. Add the shiitake mushrooms and continue to cook until softened, about 4 minutes. Add the sausage and wine and bring to a boil. Stir in the rice, soy sauce and Chicken Stock. Taste for seasoning and add salt if necessary. Bring mixture to a boil, stirring a few times. Cover rice and reduce heat to low until the rice is tender and all the stock is absorbed, about 12 minutes. Let rice stand for 5 minutes covered. Stir in the chopped cilantro and serve.

Chinese sausage is a preserved sausage that is made from diced pork, pork liver and duck liver. It is very rich and a little goes a long way.

Smoky Succotash

2 tablespoons olive oil

¼ pound bacon, ¼" dice

⅓ cup red onion, small diced

⅓ cup red pepper, small diced

2 cups fresh corn kernels

2 teaspoons jalapeño, small diced

1 cup garbanzo beans, drained and rinsed

1 cup edamame beans

1½ teaspoons Brown Sugar BBQ Rub, page 178

⅓ cup heavy cream

Kosher salt

Black pepper

Fresh parsley, chopped

Sauté the bacon in olive oil for about 6-7 minutes until bacon starts to crisp. Add the red onion and red pepper and continue to cook for 3-4 minutes more. Add the corn and jalapeño and continue to cook for an additional 3-4 minutes. Add the garbanzo beans, edamame beans, barbecue rub and cream and cook until hot and mixture starts to thicken. Season with salt and pepper and stir in the chopped parsley.

Sweet and Sour Cabbage

1 pound red cabbage, cut into 1" cubes

¼ pound bacon, ¼" dice

½ large red onion, julienned

½ cup red wine vinegar

½ cup apple cider vinegar

¾ brown sugar

¾ teaspoon ground cumin

1 Granny Smith apple, cut into ½" dice

Kosher salt

Black pepper

Cut the cabbage in half lengthwise and cut out the core. Cut each half in half again lengthwise, then cut each quarter crosswise into ¾ to ½ inch cubes. In a braising pan, cook the bacon until all fat is rendered and bacon start to crisp. Add the red onion and cook until soft. Add cabbage and cook for 15 minutes, stirring often. Add the vinegars, brown sugar and the cumin. Reduce heat to medium and cook for 20 minutes. Add the apple and continue to cook until cabbage is soft and liquid is thick and syrupy, about 20 more minutes. Remove from heat and season with salt and pepper.

Smokey Succotash page 166

SIDES

Sweet Thai Chili Noodles

MAKES 4-6 SERVINGS

1 pound spaghetti, dried

3 tablespoons sesame oil

⅓ cup soy sauce

½ cup sweet chili sauce

¼ cup fish sauce

2 tablespoons sweet soy sauce

1 tablespoon Sambal Olek Chili Paste

1 tablespoon green onion, sliced

Boil the spaghetti in salted water until al dente. In a large mixing bowl whisk the rest of the ingredients together until smooth. Drain spaghetti and toss HOT noodles with the dressing. Allow to cool to room temperature, tossing frequently. Serve at room temperature.

Toasted Barley Risotto

MAKES 4-6 SERVINGS

1½ cups pearl barley

3 tablespoons olive oil

1½ teaspoons garlic, minced

1 tablespoon shallot, minced

⅓ cup red wine

4 cups Beef Stock, warm, page 52

2 teaspoons honey

¾ cup Parmesan cheese

Kosher salt

Black pepper

Toast barley on a baking sheet for about 3-4 minutes until hot. Sauté the garlic and shallots in the olive oil until soft. Add the toasted barley and stir until coated with oil. Add the red wine and allow to evaporate. Add ½ cup of Beef Stock and allow to evaporate. Continue to add stock, ½ cup at a time as soon as the previous cup is absorbed, until the barley is tender, but still firm. Total cooking process is about 25 minutes. Stir in the honey and Parmesan cheese and season with salt and pepper.

Truffled Mashed Potatoes

MAKES 4-6 SERVINGS

4 cups Eddie's Garlic Mashed Potatoes, page 160

⅓ cup Truffle Butter, page 176

1 tablespoon parsley, chopped

Slowly melt the Truffle Butter over low heat. In a small mixing bowl, mix the mashed potatoes with the Truffle Butter and parsley. Blend until smooth.

Our side dishes are a big part of what we do at Eddie Merlots. We designed them to be an adventurous spin on the typical steakhouse offerings. All of our sides are meant to be shared, but are often enjoyed by some as their meals, from the macaroni and cheese to the hash browns, you will find all of our sides to be a satisfying accompaniment to our entrees.

Sweet Thai Chile Noodles page 168

Coffee Rub Crusted Lamb Chops page 180

butters and spices

Grilled Chipotle Beef Skewers with C...

Twin Filets with Truffle Butter

Bleu Cheese Butter

MAKES ¾ CUP

1 stick unsalted butter

¼ cup Maytag bleu cheese or other high quality bleu

2 teaspoons fresh thyme, chopped

1½ teaspoons Worcestershire sauce

2-3 drops hot sauce

Kosher salt

Black pepper

Cream the butter in a mixer until soft. Add the rest of the ingredients. Season with salt and pepper and continue to mix until smooth. Store refrigerated until needed, but bring to room temperature before using.

This goes great with a grilled steak with some fat, such as ribeye or New York.

Boursin Cheese Butter

MAKES ¾ CUP

1 stick unsalted butter

¼ cup Boursin cheese

2 teaspoons fresh chives, chopped

½ teaspoon fresh tarragon, chopped

Kosher salt

Black pepper

Cream the butter in a mixer until soft. Add the rest of the ingredients. Season with salt and pepper and continue to mix until smooth. Store refrigerated until needed, but bring to room temperature before using.

This goes well with any grilled game, such as lamb, elk or venison.

Chipotle Butter

MAKES 1 CUP

2 sticks unsalted butter

4 chipotle peppers, (canned en adobo)

2 tablespoons fresh cilantro leaves, chopped

1 fresh lime, zested and juiced

1 teaspoon cumin powder

Kosher salt

Black pepper

Cream the butter in a mixer until soft. Finely mince the chipotle peppers and add to the butter with the cilantro, lime juice, zest and cumin powder. Season with salt and pepper and mix until thoroughly combined. Refrigerate until needed, but bring to room temperature before using.

This butter is perfect on the Grilled Chipotle Beef Skewers, page 122, or on a grilled skirt steak.

Clarified Butter

MAKES ¾ POUND

1 pound unsalted butter

Place butter in a medium sauce pan, over medium high heat. Bring butter to a boil, this takes approximately 2-3 minutes. Once boiling, reduce heat to medium. After the water has evaporated, the milk solids will begin to fry in the clear butterfat. When they begin to turn golden, remove the pan from the heat and pour the butter through a fine strainer lined with damp cheesecloth into a heat proof container. Store in an airtight container being sure to keep free from moisture. Clarified

Butter does not need refrigeration and will keep in an airtight container for up to one month.

Clarified butter has had the milk solids and water removed. One advantage of clarified butter is that it has a much higher smoke point, so you can cook with it at higher temperatures without it browning or burning. Also, without the milk solids, clarified butter can be kept for a much longer period without going rancid.

Grilled Chipotle Beef Skewers with Chipotle Butter page 172

Herbed Brown Butter

MAKES ½ CUP

1 stick unsalted butter

4 teaspoons fresh parsley, chopped

½ teaspoon fresh thyme, chopped

2 teaspoons fresh chives, chopped

½ teaspoon fresh dill, chopped

1 teaspoon fresh tarragon, chopped

Kosher salt

Black pepper

In a small sauce pan, heat the butter over medium heat until butter has melted. Continue to cook butter until it turns an amber brown color and has a very nutty smell. Make sure to pay attention to the butter when it starts to brown, it goes from golden brown to burnt very fast. Remove from heat and strain through a fine strainer to remove any burnt specks and allow butter to cool to room temperature. Whisk in the chopped herbs and season with salt and pepper. Transfer to the refrigerator, stirring often as it sets to keep the herbs from settling to the bottom. Store in the refrigerator, but allow to come to room temperature before using.

This goes well with pan fried fish, such as walleye, perch or trout.

Lobster Butter

MAKES 1 CUP

2 sticks unsalted butter, room temperature

½ teaspoon garlic clove, roasted

¾ teaspoon lobster base

½ teaspoon Tarragon Reduction, page 48

Kosher salt

Black pepper

Cream the butter in a mixer until soft. Add the rest of the ingredients. Season with salt and pepper and continue to mix until smooth. Store refrigerated until needed, but bring to room temperature before using.

This butter goes with our Lobster Mashed Potatoes, page 162, or on grilled salmon and swordfish.

Merlot Butter

MAKES ½ CUP

1 cup merlot wine

1 rosemary sprig

2 bay leaves

1 shallot, sliced

6 whole peppercorns

1 stick unsalted butter

1 teaspoon garlic clove, roasted

1 teaspoon fresh thyme, chopped

Kosher salt

Black pepper

Combine the wine with the rosemary, bay leaves, shallot and peppercorns in a small sauce pan and bring to a boil. Lower heat and simmer mixture until reduced by 75% or ¼ cup. Strain wine through a fine strainer and allow to cool to room temperature. Cream the butter and garlic in a mixer until soft. With mixer running, slowly add the wine concentrate until fully incorporated. Add the chopped thyme, season with salt and pepper and continue to mix until smooth. Store refrigerated until needed, but bring to room temperature before using.

This goes well with any bone in steak, from filets to ribeyes.

Mustard Butter

MAKES ½ CUP

1 stick unsalted butter

2½ teaspoons Dijon mustard

⅛ teaspoon granulated garlic

⅛ teaspoon onion powder

Pinch turmeric

¼ teaspoon Tabasco sauce

1½ teaspoon whole grain mustard

Kosher salt

Cream the butter in a mixer until soft. Add the rest of the ingredients. Season with salt and pepper and continue to mix until smooth. Store refrigerated until needed, but bring to room temperature before using.

This butter goes well with grilled chicken and great on sourdough bread.

Surf and Turf with Lobster Butter page 174

Spinach Butter

MAKES ½ CUP

1½ teaspoons shallot, minced

1½ teaspoons garlic, minced

1 bay leaf

¼ cup dry white wine

½ cup fresh spinach, chopped

1 stick unsalted butter

Kosher salt

White pepper

In a small sauce pan, combine the shallots, garlic, bay leaf and white wine. Bring to a boil, reduce heat to a simmer and cook until almost dry, leaving a bit of liquid. Remove from heat and while still warm, add the spinach and stir until spinach is wilted and soft. Set mixture aside and allow to cool to room temperature. In a mixer, cream the butter until soft. Fold in the spinach mixture, season with salt and pepper and continue to mix until all ingredients are thoroughly combined. Store refrigerated until needed, but bring to room temperature before using.

This butter is used for our sautéed spinach and would work well in sprucing up a baked potato.

Steak Butter

MAKES 1 CUP

¾ teaspoon shallot, minced

¾ teaspoon Clarified Butter, page 172

2 sticks unsalted butter

1 teaspoon garlic clove, roasted

1-2 drops Tabasco sauce

¾ teaspoon Worcestershire sauce

½ teaspoon fresh lemon juice

¾ teaspoon fresh parsley, minced

Kosher salt

White pepper

In a small sauté pan, gently cook the shallots in the Clarified Butter just until soft. Remove from heat and allow mixture to cool to room temperature. In a mixer, cream the butter until soft and add the shallots and the rest of the ingredients. Season with salt and pepper and continue to mix until all ingredients are thoroughly combined. Store refrigerated until needed, but bring to room temperature before using.

This is great brushed on any steak and also makes a great picatta sauce for chicken or fish.

Tapenade Butter

MAKES ⅔ CUP

2 tablespoons assorted olives, pitted, rough chop

¼ teaspoon fresh lemon zest

1 teaspoon capers

1 anchovy fillet

¼ teaspoon garlic, minced

Pinch crushed red pepper

1 stick unsalted butter, cut into cubes

Kosher salt

Black pepper

Combine the olives, lemon zest, capers, anchovy, garlic and crushed red pepper in a food processor and pulse 4-5 times until mixture is coarsely ground. Add the butter, season with salt and pepper and pulse again, just until combined. Store butter refrigerated until needed, but bring to room temperature before using.

This goes on the Tuscan grilled New York strip, but is equally good on chicken.

Truffle Butter

MAKES ½ CUP

1 stick unsalted butter

¾ teaspoon black truffle peelings, minced

1 tablespoon white truffle oil

¼ teaspoon fresh chives, minced

Kosher salt

Black pepper

Cream the butter in a mixer until soft. Add the black truffle peelings, truffle oil and chives. Season with salt and pepper and continue to mix until smooth. Store refrigerated until needed, but bring to room temperature before using.

Truffles are an underground mushroom style fungus that grow on the roots of specific varieties of trees. The flavor of truffles is directly tied to their aroma which has a strong, pungent, earthy and almost barnyard like quality that can only be described as "intoxicating".

This butter goes with anything from roast chicken to prime rib.

Twin Filets with Truffle Butter page 176

Blackened Spice

MAKES ¾ CUP

2 tablespoons Hungarian paprika

2 tablespoons basil leaves, dried

1 tablespoon oregano leaves, dried

1 tablespoon granulated garlic

1 tablespoon onion powder

1 tablespoon cayenne pepper

1 tablespoon black pepper

1 tablespoon kosher salt

1 tablespoon sugar

1 tablespoon thyme leaves, dried

Combine all ingredients together into a food processor and pulse until thoroughly combined. Keep covered in a cool, dry place.

Brown Sugar BBQ Rub

MAKES ¾ CUP

½ cup brown sugar

1½ teaspoons cayenne pepper

3 tablespoons kosher salt

1½ teaspoons black pepper

1 teaspoon ground cumin

½ teaspoon thyme leaves, dried

½ teaspoon onion powder

½ teaspoon Old Bay seasoning

1 tablespoon Blackened Spice

Combine all ingredients together into a food processor and pulse until thoroughly combined. Keep covered in a cool, dry place.

Caribbean Jerk Spice

MAKES ½ CUP

2 tablespoons kosher salt

1¾ teaspoons allspice

2 tablespoons brown sugar

1¾ teaspoons garlic powder

1¾ teaspoons granulated onion

¾ teaspoon cayenne pepper

1 teaspoon paprika

1 teaspoon chives, dried

¾ teaspoon nutmeg

1 teaspoon black pepper

¾ teaspoon ground ginger

½ teaspoon ground cinnamon

½ teaspoon ground cloves

½ teaspoon thyme, dried

2 teaspoons sugar

Combine all ingredients together into a food processor and pulse until thoroughly combined. Keep covered in a cool, dry place.

New York Strip with Blackened Spice page 178

Chicken Rub

MAKES 1 CUP

3 tablespoons paprika

2 tablespoons basil leaves, dried

4 teaspoons oregano leaves, dried

4 teaspoons rosemary leaves, dried

2 tablespoons thyme leaves, dried

4 teaspoons granulated garlic

4 teaspoons onion salt

4 teaspoons black pepper

4 teaspoons kosher salt

4 teaspoons sugar

Combine all ingredients together into a food processor and pulse until thoroughly combined. Keep covered in a cool, dry place.

Coffee Rub

MAKES 1 CUP

¼ cup freshly ground coffee

2 tablespoons kosher salt

1 tablespoon crushed red pepper

2 tablespoons black pepper

1 tablespoon garlic, minced

¼ cup sugar

Mix all ingredients together and store, covered, in the refrigerator.

Steak Seasoning I

MAKES ¾ CUP

½ cup course sea salt

¼ cup cracked black pepper

This is the recipe we use at the restaurant. The reason it's so simple is that we buy the highest quality beef we can, and we want to highlight the flavor of the beef itself without masking any of its subtle flavors.

Eddie's Bread Seasoning

MAKES 1 CUP

1 cup Parmesan cheese, grated

6 tablespoons paprika

2 tablespoons granulated garlic

2 tablespoons kosher salt

2 tablespoons Herbs de Provence

Place all ingredients into a food processor and pulse until thoroughly combined. Store, covered, in the refrigerator.

Steak Seasoning II

MAKES 1 CUP

2 tablespoons onion salt

2 tablespoons garlic salt

2 tablespoons onion powder

2 tablespoons ground black pepper

2 tablespoons Hungarian paprika

2 tablespoons sugar

2 tablespoons kosher salt

2 tablespoons celery salt

This recipe is one that can be used to spice up a steak to give it a little more punch or flavor. It is equally good on pork chops and chicken.

Bread with Eddie's Bread Seasoning page 180

Coconut Cream Pie page 196

desserts

Classic Creme Brulee

Caramel Macchiato Cake

Red Velvet Cake

Apple and Peach Crisp

MAKES 6-8 SERVINGS

8 cups Granny Smith apples, peeled, cored and sliced

2 cups peaches, cored and sliced

1 cup granulated sugar

2 teaspoons ground cinnamon

⅓ teaspoon ground nutmeg

Pinch ground allspice

2 tablespoons corn starch

1 cup Apple Butter, page 34

½ teaspoon kosher salt

2 tablespoons brandy

1 recipe Apple Crisp Crust

Vanilla Crème Anglaise, page 200

Cinnamon Ice Cream

Preheat oven to 375 degrees. In a large mixing bowl combine all the ingredients except crust and put into a buttered 9x12" baking pan. Cover the apple mixture with the crust and bake in the oven for 30-35 minutes until apples are soft and crust is golden brown. Serve hot with the crème anglaise or room temperature with ice cream.

Applewood Bacon Brittle

MAKES ½ SHEET TRAY

2 cups granulated sugar

1 cup light corn syrup

½ cup water

1 teaspoons kosher salt

2 tablespoons cold bacon grease

1 tablespoon unsalted butter, cut into cubes

2 teaspoons baking soda

1 cup applewood smoked bacon pieces, cooked crispy

In a heavy bottom sauce pan, bring the first four ingredients to a boil and cook until at the hard crack stage, swirling the pan to distribute heat (300-310 degrees on a candy thermometer). Remove mixture from heat and quickly stir in the bacon grease, butter and baking soda. Keep stirring until butter has melted. Fold in the cooked bacon pieces and spread the brittle mixture onto a parchment paper lined ½ sheet pan and allow to cool to room temperature. When cooled, break into small pieces and store in an airtight container at room temperature.

Apple Spice Cake

MAKES 8 SERVINGS

4 cups flour

2 teaspoons baking soda

1 teaspoon kosher salt

1 teaspoon ground cinnamon

1 teaspoon ground nutmeg

1 teaspoon white pepper

1 teaspoon ground allspice

1 teaspoon ground cloves

8 large eggs, room temperature, lightly beaten

⅔ cup sour cream, room temperature

⅔ cup molasses

2 teaspoons ginger, peeled, finely grated

2 tablespoons fresh lemon zest

1 pound unsalted butter, melted

2⅔ cups light brown sugar

4 Granny Smith apples, peeled and cored

8 tablespoons light brown sugar

1 batch Brie Cheese and Honey Icing, page 186

Kentucky Bourbon Sauce, page 198

Preheat oven to 350 degrees. In a small mixing bowl, mix together the first 8 ingredients. In another small mixing bowl mix the eggs, sour cream and the molasses and whisk until smooth. Pour the wet mixture into the dry mixture and whisk until smooth. Fold in the ginger, lemon zest, melted butter and the first quantity of brown sugar and mix until smooth. Continued on page 186.

Apple Crisp Crust

MAKES 4 CUPS

2 sticks unsalted butter, softened

1 cup brown sugar

2 cups flour

1 cup uncooked oats

Mix all ingredients together by hand, leaving visible lumps of butter and sugar. Put into a plastic storage container with a tight lid and store in refrigerator until needed.

Apple Spice Cake page 184

Apple Spice Cake

CONTINUED

Lightly butter 8 individual spring form pans and sprinkle the bottom of each with 1 tablespoon of brown sugar. Slice the apples into ⅛" thick slices and evenly fan around the bottom of the pans. Fill the spring form pans with the batter ¾ of the way full and bake in the oven for 30-40 minutes or until toothpick comes out clean. Remove cakes from the oven and cool on a cooling rack. Cut the tops of the cakes off flush with the top of the spring form pans. Unmold each cake and put the Brie Cheese and Honey Icing into a pastry bag. Turn the cakes upside down and pip a generous amount of the frosting on top of each cake. Serve cakes at room temperature with the Kentucky Bourbon Sauce.

Brie Cheese and Honey Icing

MAKES 4 CUPS

1 pound soft variety brie cheese, rind removed, room temperature

6 ounces unsalted butter, room temperature

3 cups Cream Cheese Frosting, page 196

2 tablespoons honey

Banana Cream Pie

MAKES 8 SERVINGS

8 4½" individual pastry shells, baked

40 fresh banana slices

1 batch Banana Pastry Cream

8 cups whipped cream

Toasted almond slices

Homemade Caramel Sauce, page 192

Peanut Brittle, page 198

Mint sprigs

Place the pastry shells on a cookie sheet and place 5 slices of banana in the bottom of each shell. Divide the pastry cream evenly among the pie shells and top each with some of the whipped cream. Place the pie in the refrigerator until ready to serve. Sprinkle the almonds over the top of the pies when ready to serve. Serve with a generous amount of Caramel Sauce and some Peanut Brittle on the side for texture.

Using a stand mixer with the paddle attachment, beat the brie cheese and the butter until smooth, about 4 minutes. Scrape down the sides of the bowl with a rubber spatula and add the Cream Cheese Frosting and the honey and continue to mix until smooth, about 3 more minutes. Transfer frosting to the refrigerator for about 10 minutes to firm slightly before using.

The brie cheese in this icing makes it wonderful on any fruit cake style dessert. Try it with a pear or peach upside down cake for a great flavor combination.

Banana Pastry Cream

MAKES 4½ CUPS

½ cup corn starch

1⅓ cups whole milk

1⅓ cups Half & Half

1 cup granulated sugar

3 whole eggs, large

3 egg yolks, large

6 ounces unsalted butter, cut into cubes

2 teaspoons pure vanilla extract

3 tablespoons banana liqueur

In a mixing bowl whisk together the corn starch with the milk. In a medium sauce pan, bring the Half & Half and the sugar to a boil. Mix the eggs and egg yolks into the corn starch mixture. Temper the hot milk with the egg mixture and slowly mix back into the hot milk. Continue to cook over medium low heat, whisking constantly, until the mixture thickens and is the consistency of a thick pudding. Remove from heat and fold in the butter, vanilla and banana liqueur. Pass pastry cream through a strainer, while still warm, into a storage container and cover with plastic wrap directly on the surface. Place in the refrigerator to firm, about 3 hours, before serving.

Banana Cream Pie page 186

Bananas Foster

MAKES 4 SERVINGS

4 bananas, ripe

½ cup unsalted butter

1 cup brown sugar

3 ounces dark rum

3 ounces banana liqueur

Pinch cinnamon

4 vanilla bean ice cream balls, very, very cold

Peel and split the bananas lengthwise down the middle. Cut them crosswise also so you have 4 slices per banana. Set aside. In a large sauté pan, over medium heat, melt the butter and the brown sugar, stirring constantly until the sugar dissolves, about 2 minutes. Add the bananas and the banana liqueur and bring to a simmer for 1 minute, stirring often. Turn heat to high and, carefully tilting the pan away from you, add the rum and flame. If it does not light, turn heat down slightly and carefully light with a long stick lighter. Turn down heat to low and sprinkle the pan with a liberal amount of cinnamon, creating a shower of "sparks". Baste the bananas with the syrup for 15-20 seconds. Place each ice cream ball into individual bowls and spoon four slices of bananas over each bowl of ice cream. Spoon the sauce around the ice cream and serve immediately.

Blackberry Cobbler

MAKES 6-8 SERVINGS

10 cups fresh blackberries

4 cups granulated sugar

4 cups flour

4 teaspoons baking powder

1 teaspoon salt

2½ cups milk

1 cup unsalted butter, melted

3 tablespoons granulated sugar

Preheat oven to 375 degrees. In a medium mixing bowl toss the blackberries with the first amount of sugar and allow to stand for 20 minutes until syrup starts to form. Pour the mixture into a 9"x12" baking dish. Mix the rest of the ingredients in a mixing bowl, just until blended, do not over mix. Pour the batter over the berries and bake in the oven for 30-40 minutes until the dough has risen and is golden brown. Remove from oven and allow to cool for 20 minutes to give the fruit a chance to set before serving.

You don't have to use only blackberries for this recipe. You can use just about any combination of fruit. We sometimes mix raspberries in with this and serve with mint ice cream.

Bourbon Pecan Toffee Pie

MAKES 2 PIES

4 Heath bars

3 cups whipping cream

1 tablespoon instant coffee (diluted in a small amount of hot water)

1 can sweetened condensed milk

6 tablespoons Kentucky bourbon

12 ounces toasted pecan pieces

2 graham cracker pie shells

Caramel Sauce, page 192

Chop Heath bars into small bite size pieces and set aside. Using a stand mixer with a whip attachment, whip the cream until soft peaks are formed. Fold in the diluted coffee, sweetened condensed milk and the bourbon. Fold in half of the Heath bar pieces and half of the pecan pieces. Fill both graham cracker shells evenly with the filling. Sprinkle the remaining Heath pieces and pecans over the top of the pies and freeze until hard, about 3 hours. Serve frozen with Caramel Sauce.

Blackberry Cobbler page 188

Campfire S'mores Tart

MAKES 10 SERVINGS

3 cups graham cracker crumbs

½ cup granulated sugar

1 stick unsalted butter, melted

Crust: Preheat oven to 350 degrees. In a small mixing bowl, combine the graham cracker crumbs, sugar and melted butter. Mix well. Lightly spray 10 mini spring form pans with non-stick spray and portion ⅓ cup of crust into each pan. Bake crust in the oven for 8 minutes. Remove crusts from oven and let cool.

1 pound semisweet chocolate chips

½ pound unsalted butter

⅓ cup hazelnut liqueur

8 whole eggs

¼ cup granulated sugar

1 teaspoon pure vanilla extract

½ teaspoon kosher salt

Filling: Combine chocolate chips, butter and the liqueur in a small stainless steel mixing bowl and set over a pan of barely simmering water. Whisk mixture until smooth and set aside. In another small mixing bowl, whip eggs, sugar, vanilla and salt until pale and slightly thickened. Gently fold the melted chocolate mixture into the whipped eggs a little at a time until fully incorporated. Spoon ¾ cup of the batter into each spring form pan with the crusts. Reduce oven temperature to 325 degrees and bake cakes for 15-20 minutes or until a wooden skewer comes out clean. Remove cakes and allow to cool completely.

Campfire S'mores Tart

CONTINUED

Marshmallow Fluff

Mini Marshmallows

Caramel Sauce, page 192

Topping: Finish the cakes by unmolding and spreading a thin and even layer of marshmallow fluff over each cake. Arrange an even layer of mini marshmallows over the fluff, making sure to cover the entire surface. Right before serving, use a blow torch and carefully toast the top of the marshmallows and serve with the Caramel Sauce on the side.

Caramel Macchiato Cake

MAKES 10-12 SERVINGS

12 ounce white cake mix, basic boxed

½ cup sour cream

¼ cup water

2 tablespoons canola oil

2 eggs, large

½ cup Kahlua

½ cup Caramel Sauce, page 192

1¼ cups espresso, freshly brewed

Cake: Preheat oven to 350 degrees. With an electric mixer, combine cake mix, sour cream, water, oil and eggs and blend with the whip attachment for 2-4 minutes. Be sure to scrape the sides of the bowl while mixing. Liberally spray a ¼ sheet cake pan with extended sides with nonstick spray and pour the batter into the pan. Bake in the oven for 20-25 minutes or until a wooden pick inserted in the center comes out clean.

Caramel Macchiato Cake

CONTINUED

Remove from oven and let the cake cool. In a small mixing bowl, combine the Kahlua, Caramel Sauce and espresso together and pour this mixture evenly over the cooled cake. Place the cake in the refrigerator while making the mousse.

1 pound semisweet chocolate chips

¼ pound unsalted butter

6 large eggs, separated

1 cup granulated sugar

1 teaspoon pure vanilla extract

1 cup heavy cream

Mousse: Melt the chocolate and butter in a metal mixing bowl over a pan of barely simmering water and allow mixture to come to room temperature. In another small metal mixing bowl, cook the egg yolks, ½ cup sugar and vanilla over the same pot of barely simmering water, stirring constantly until thick like pudding. Add the egg mixture to the chocolate mixture. Using an electric mixer with a whip attachment, whip the heavy cream to medium peaks and gently fold into the chocolate egg mixture. Clean out the mixing bowl and whip the egg whites to medium peaks and, with the mixer still running, slowly add ½ cup sugar until fully incorporated. Gently fold the egg whites into the mousse, being careful not to over mix. Spread the mousse evenly over the top of the cake. Transfer cake to the freezer to set, about 4 hours. While still frozen, cut the cake into serving pieces and transfer back to the refrigerator until ready to serve. Keep any leftovers refrigerated for up to 5 days.

Caramel Macciato Cake page 190

Caramel Sauce

MAKES 1½ CUPS

9 ounces granulated sugar

¼ cup water

2 teaspoons fresh lemon juice

1 cup heavy cream

4 tablespoons unsalted butter

In a clean and dry heavy bottomed sauce pan, combine the sugar and the water and bring to a boil. Add the lemon juice and continue to boil without stirring until sugar reaches 365 degrees on a candy thermometer. Remove from heat and carefully whisk in the cream and then the butter. Continue to whisk until smooth.

Carrot Cake

MAKES 8-10 SERVINGS

½ pound golden raisins

¾ pound pineapple tidbits, canned

½ cup walnut pieces

1½ pound carrots, peeled

1 pound canola oil

1½ pounds sugar

¾ pound whole eggs

4 teaspoons kosher salt

4 teaspoons ground cinnamon

2 teaspoons baking soda

3 teaspoons baking powder

Carrot Cake

CONTINUED

1 pound flour

¾ teaspoon ground allspice

¾ teaspoon ground cloves

6 cups Cream Cheese Frosting, room temperature, page 196

Preheat oven to 400 degrees. Cover raisins with very hot tap water and soak for 30 minutes, drain completely and set aside. Squeeze all moisture from pineapple tidbits. In a food processor, chop the pineapple, walnuts and carrots into small ⅛" pieces and set aside. Weigh out and measure all other ingredients and have ready. Using a stand mixer, with a paddle attachment, alternately add oil and sugar together. Mix at low speed until sugar is dissolved. Add the eggs in 3 separate batches until completely incorporated. With the motor still running, add all of the dry ingredients and mix, scraping down bowl frequently. Fold in reserved pineapple, carrots, raisins and walnuts. Spray 2 half sheet trays with non-stick spray, line with parchment paper and spray again. Pour half the cake batter evenly in to each pan. Bake in the oven for 25 minutes or until a skewer inserted into the center comes out clean. Remove from oven and let cool to room temperature. Trim the edges from each cake and cut each in half to achieve 4 equal pieces. Spread 1½ cups of frosting on the first layer of the cake and top with another cake layer. Repeat this step for the third and fourth layers using 1½ cups of icing between each layer.

Chocolate Pots de Crème

MAKES 7 SERVINGS

2 cups Half & Half

2 cups heavy cream

12 ounces semisweet chocolate chips

12 ounces granulated sugar

½ tablespoon vanilla extract

¾ cup egg yolks

Whipped cream

Chocolate curls

Fresh mint sprigs

Powdered sugar

Preheat oven to 325 degrees. In a medium sauce pan, heat the Half & Half and the cream to a simmer, being careful not to boil over. Turn off heat and add the chocolate chips and whisk until mixture is smooth. In a medium mixing bowl, combine sugar, vanilla and egg yolks and beat until pale and creamy. Gradually whisk the hot chocolate and cream mixture into the egg mixture and strain through a fine sieve. Divide the custard into 7 individual 8-ounce ramekins. Place ramekins into a baking dish and fill dish with hot water to come halfway up the sides. Bake custards in the oven for 50 minutes or until just barely set. Carefully remove pan from the oven and allow to cool. When cool remove the ramekins from the water bath and place in the refrigerator until completely chilled, about 3 hours. When ready to serve, garnish the tops of each Pots de Crème with a small dollop of whipped cream, a sprinkling of chocolate curls, a mint sprig and a dusting of powdered sugar.

Carrot Cake page 192

Christmas Mud Pie

MAKES 1 PIE

1 pre-made Oreo cookie crust shell

½ cup Gooey Fudge Sauce, page 198

½ gallon mint chocolate ice cream

1½ gallons peppermint ice cream

Crushed candy canes

Spoon half of the fudge sauce into the bottom of the Oreo cookie pie shell. Cut the peppermint and chocolate ice cream tubs in half vertically with a large 2 handled knife. Then cut the halves into ½" thick slices. (Do not do this too far ahead). Place two ½" slices of the mint chocolate ice cream on top off the fudge in the pie pan. Place three more ½" slices of mint chocolate ice cream standing up to make sides of the mud pie. Put pie in freezer until firm. Remove pie from freezer. Fill inside of pie with chunks of peppermint ice cream and the remaining fudge (do not leave spaces). On the outside of the pie put pieces of peppermint ice cream to cover the mint chocolate ice cream. Smooth the outside with a spatula, cover with plastic wrap and place in the freezer for 4 hours until hard. When ready to serve, remove plastic wrap and cut into 8 pieces. Garnish with a sprinkling of crushed candy canes.

Citrus Semifreddo

MAKES 5 SERVINGS

½ cup granulated sugar

5 egg yolks

¼ cup fresh lemon juice

3 tablespoons fresh lime juice

2 tablespoons Limon Cello

Pinch kosher salt

1 lemon, zested

1 lime, zested

1 cup heavy cream

¼ cup granulated sugar

5 3"wide x 2" tall P.V.C. molds

1 heaping cup whipped cream

5 tablespoons crushed amaretto cookies

1½ cups fresh sliced raspberries

5 fresh mint sprigs

Whisk ½ cup sugar, egg yolks, lemon and lime juices, Limon Cello and salt in a large mixing bowl. Cook over a pot of simmering water, stirring constantly, until mixture reaches 160 degrees and is thick and creamy. Whisk the lemon and lime zests into the custard. Remove from heat and let cool. Whip the heavy cream to soft peaks and gradually add ¼ cup sugar. Continue to whip until stiff peaks are formed. Fold whipped cream into custard a little at a time. Line 5 3" PVC pipe ring molds with a strip of parchment paper. Place on a baking tray lined with parchment paper. Pipe ¾ cup custard into each mold. Place finished custards into the freezer for 8 hours or overnight. To serve, push custards out of ring molds and remove the parchment strip. Place custards on individual serving plates and top each with whipped cream. Sprinkle the crushed cookies over the custards and garnish with the sliced raspberries and mint sprigs.

Classic Crème Brulee

MAKES 4 SERVINGS

5 ounces egg yolks

½ cup sugar

3 cups whipping cream

1-2 drops vanilla extract

1 vanilla bean, split and scraped

8 teaspoons light brown sugar

2 cups fresh berries

Preheat oven to 325 degrees. In a medium sauce pan, combine the heavy cream, vanilla extract and vanilla bean and bring mixture to a simmer over medium heat. Remove from heat and let sit for 10 minutes. In a small mixing bowl, whip sugar and egg yolks together until pale and creamy. Slowly ladle a small amount of the hot cream mixture into the egg yolks while whisking. Continue to do this until both mixtures are combined. Strain custard through a fine sieve. Portion batter into 4 8-ounce crème brulee dishes and place into a large baking dish. Pour enough water into the baking dish to go half way up the sides of the dishes. Bake in the oven for 30 minutes, rotate pan and finish baking for an additional 15-20 minutes, until just barely set. Remove pan from oven and carefully drain hot water from baking dish. Allow custards to cool to room temperature and transfer to the refrigerator until fully chilled, about 3 hours. When ready to serve, sprinkle each custard with 2 teaspoons brown sugar and tilt dish to completely cover the top. Using a propane torch, lightly toast the sugar until an even golden brown. Allow custards to cool for 2 minutes and serve with fresh berries.

Classic Créme Brulee page 194

Coconut Cream Pie

MAKES 6 SERVINGS

1   12-ounce box vanilla wafers

½   pound sugar

½   pound unsalted butter, melted

Preheat oven to 350 degrees. Crush vanilla wafers in a food processor. Add sugar and butter and pulse to combine. Press ½ cup crust mixture into each of 6 individual spring form pans, making sure the crust goes up the sides and is not too thick on the bottom. Bake crust for 10 minutes, remove from oven and cool to room temperature.

4   cups Half & Half

2   cups sugar

1½   cups flour

2   cups coconut flakes

1   teaspoon vanilla extract

1½   cups egg yolk

Bring 3 cups Half & Half and sugar to a simmer in a medium sauce pan. Whisk together the other cup of Half & Half with the flour, coconut, vanilla and egg yolks. Slowly whisk the hot milk into the milk/flour mixture. Pour mixture back into sauce pan and cook over medium heat, stirring constantly, until thick and eggs are cooked. Divide custard evenly among the pie shells and chill in the refrigerator for 4-5 hours.

Whipped cream topping

Toasted coconut flakes

Caramel Sauce, page 192

To serve, unmold pies and generously top with whipped cream. Sprinkle with toasted coconut and drizzle Caramel Sauce over the top.

Cream Cheese Frosting

MAKES 4 CUPS

1¼   pound powdered sugar

10   ounces cream cheese, room temperature

5   ounces unsalted butter, room temperature

1   teaspoon vanilla extract

Pinch kosher salt

Using a stand mixer with paddle, combine the cream cheese and butter on medium speed, just until blended. Stop and scrape down the sides of the bowl. Add the vanilla and salt and beat until combined. With the speed on low, add the powdered sugar in 4 batches, beating until smooth between each addition. Refrigerate for 5-10 minutes before using.

Crème Brulee French Toast

MAKES 8 SERVINGS

1   quart heavy cream

1   vanilla bean, split

8   egg yolks, large

1   cup granulated sugar

1   2 pound loaf soft texture egg bread

Granulated sugar

Crème Brulee French Toast

CONTINUED

Vanilla Crème Anglaise, page 200

Caramel Sauce, page 192

Maple syrup

Fresh raspberries

Cinnamon ice cream

Line a 10" spring form pan with a large sheet of foil, making sure to fully cover the inside of the pan without any holes. In a medium sauce pan, combine the cream and vanilla bean and bring to a simmer over medium heat. Turn off heat and whisk in the sugar. Allow cream to cool for half an hour and whisk in egg yolks. Strain the custard through a fine sieve and set aside. Preheat oven to 325 degrees. Cut bread loaf into 1" thick slices and make a layer of bread slices in the bottom of the spring form pan. Cut and tear slices as needed to fit. Pour 25% of the custard over the bread and repeat with 3 more layers of bread and custard. Keep the sides of the foil standing up to keep cream inside the pan until the bread absorbs it all. Allow to sit on the counter for 1 hour. Place the French toast in a water bath and bake for 1½-2 hours until just barely set. Allow to cool to room temperature and refrigerate overnight. Carefully unmold the French toast from the pan and turn upside down on a large dinner plate. Cut into 8 slices and heat as needed in the microwave until warm. Sprinkle the top of a slice with sugar and, using a propane torch, lightly caramelize the sugar until it is golden brown. Serve with some of the crème anglaise, Caramel Sauce, maple syrup, fresh raspberries and cinnamon ice cream.

Créme Brulee French Toast page 196

DESSERTS

Gooey Fudge Sauce

MAKES 3½ CUPS

2 cups sugar

4 tablespoons flour

⅔ cup cocoa powder

2 teaspoons kosher salt

2 cups milk

4 tablespoons unsalted butter

2 teaspoons vanilla

In a medium bowl, whisk together the dry ingredients. Over medium heat combine milk, butter and vanilla until the butter has melted. Add dry ingredients to the milk mixture, constantly whisking. Bring to a boil, stirring constantly, until thick and smooth, about 5 minutes. Remove from heat. Cool and refrigerate any unused portion.

Kentucky Bourbon Sauce

MAKES 2 CUPS

1 cup sugar

3 tablespoons unsalted butter

½ cup buttermilk

¼ cup Kentucky bourbon

½ teaspoon baking soda

1 tablespoon light corn syrup

1 teaspoon pure vanilla extract

Combine all ingredients in a small sauce pan and bring to a boil. Reduce heat to a simmer and cook for 1 minute. Remove from heat and cool completely. Sauce can be served warm or chilled. Refrigerate leftovers up to 7 days.

Peanut Brittle

MAKES 1 HALF SHEET PAN

2 cups granulated sugar

1 cup light corn syrup

½ cup water

1 teaspoon kosher salt

3 cups roasted peanuts, unsalted

3 tablespoons unsalted butter, cut into cubes

2 teaspoons baking soda

In a heavy bottom sauce pan, bring the first four ingredients to a boil. Add the peanuts and cook until hard crack stage, (300-310 degrees on a candy thermometer), swirling the pan to distribute heat. Remove mixture from heat and quickly stir in the butter and baking soda. Keep stirring until butter has melted. Spread brittle mixture onto a parchment lined ½ sheet pan and allow to cool to room temperature. When cooled, break into small pieces and store in an air tight container at room temperature.

This recipe is from Chef Matt's Dad. It is always a hit around the holidays, but it is equally delicious anytime with homemade ice cream.

Raspberry Sauce

MAKES 1¼ CUPS

2½ pints fresh raspberries

¼ cup water

½ cup granulated sugar

1 tablespoon corn starch

In a small pan, bring all ingredients to a boil; reduce heat to simmer and cook for 3-4 minutes. Strain to remove any seeds and chill one hour before using.

Peanut Butter Cup

MAKES 5 SERVINGS

5 3"wide x 2" tall P.V.C. molds

¾ cup ground Peanut Brittle

¾ cup graham cracker crumbs

¼ cup melted unsalted butter

¼ cup coconut flakes

Crust: Prep 5 3"x2" PVC molds by cutting strips of parchment paper to fit inside the molds. Prepare the crust by placing all ingredients into a food processor and pulse 3-4 times to combine. Divide the crust evenly into the bottoms of each ring mold and press with the back of a spoon until smooth.

4 tablespoons unsalted butter

1 cup peanut butter

¾ teaspoon vanilla extract

1 cup powdered sugar

Filling: Prepare the filling by creaming the butter in a mixer until smooth. Add the rest of the filling ingredients and continue to beat on medium high until mousse is light and fluffy, about 10 minutes. Place mousse into a pastry bag and pipe into the ring molds, being careful to eliminate as much air as possible from the molds.

3 ounces semisweet chocolate chips

2 tablespoons heavy cream

1 tablespoon unsalted butter

Topping: Prepare topping by melting all ingredients in a small mixing bowl over a pot of barely simmering water. Top each mold with the chocolate mixture and place in refrigerator for 2 hours to firm before serving.

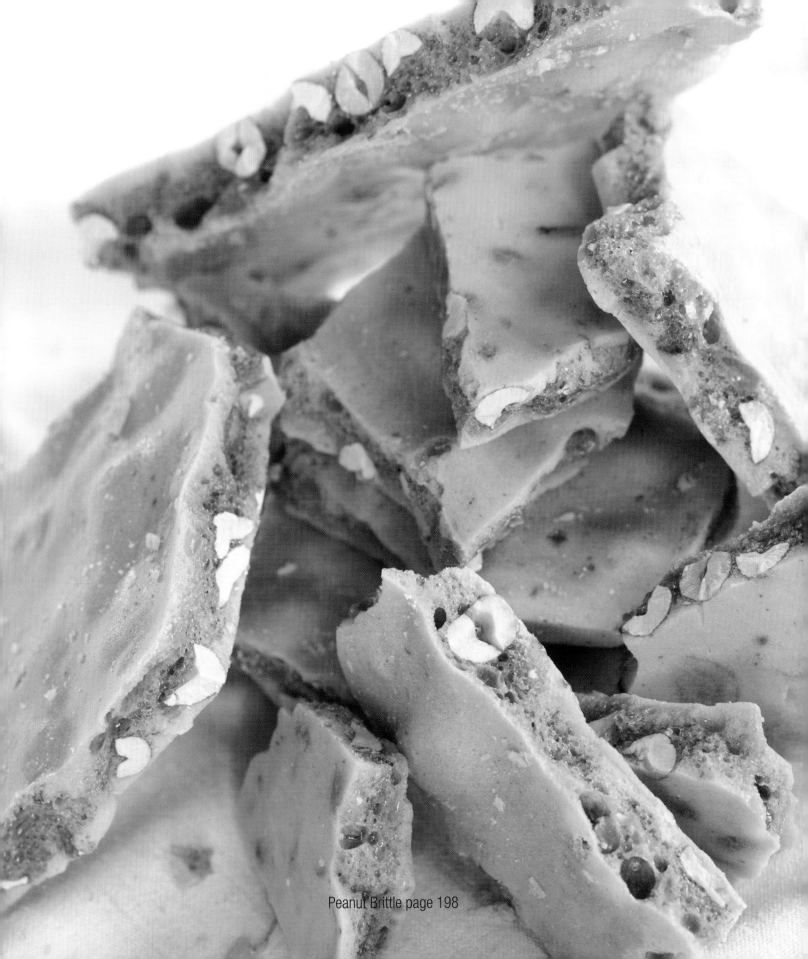

Peanut Brittle page 198

Red Velvet Cake

MAKES 8-10 SERVINGS

5½ ounces flour

4 ounces cake flour

½ ounce cocoa powder

1 teaspoon baking soda

½ teaspoon kosher salt

1 cup buttermilk

2 tablespoons red food coloring

1 teaspoon vanilla extract

3 tablespoons vegetable oil

¼ cup sour cream

10 ½ ounces light brown sugar

4 ounces unsalted butter, softened

2 whole eggs

¾ cup heavy cream

3 tablespoons Chambord liqueur

1 batch Cream Cheese Frosting,
page 196

Preheat oven to 325 degrees.
Spray 2 9-inch spring form pans
with nonstick spray. Whisk flours,
cocoa, baking soda and salt
together. In another mixing bowl
whisk buttermilk, food coloring,
vanilla, vegetable oil and sour
cream. In a stand mixer combine
brown sugar and butter and cream
on medium speed for 2 minutes.
With the mixer running, slowly add
the eggs and beat until fully
incorporated. Reduce mixer speed
to low and slowly add the flour
mixture in 3 installments, alternating
with buttermilk mixture. Continue
to mix just until smooth. Divide the
batter between the prepared pans
and bake in the oven for 30-35
minutes until a toothpick comes out
clean. Remove from oven. Mix
heavy cream and Chambord
together and brush over the cakes
while still warm. Allow cakes to
cool completely before unmolding
and icing.

Shortbread Cookies

MAKES 40 COOKIES

1½ pounds unsalted butter, softened

2 cups granulated sugar

2 teaspoons pure vanilla extract

7 cups flour

½ teaspoon kosher salt

Using a mixer, beat the butter and
sugar together until combined. Add
the vanilla, flour and salt and mix on
low speed until dough comes
together. Dump dough onto a
floured work surface and shape into
4 flat discs. Wrap each disc in
plastic and refrigerate for 30
minutes. Place dough back on
floured work surface and roll each
disc out to ½" thick and cut into
desire shapes. Place cookies on an
ungreased baking tray for 20
minutes until edges just start to
brown. Cool before storing in an
airtight container. Store in a cool
place for 4-5 days.

Vanilla Crème Anglaise

MAKES 2½ CUPS

2 cups heavy cream

1 vanilla bean

3 fresh egg yolks

½ cup granulated sugar

¼ teaspoon pure vanilla extract

Triple Berry Pie

MAKES 10 SERVINGS

10 4" pie shells, baked

1 quart strawberries, stemmed and
sliced

2½ pints fresh blueberries

2½ pints fresh raspberries

4 tablespoons Grand Marnier

1 cup brown sugar

6 tablespoons corn starch

1 teaspoon ground cinnamon

½ teaspoon pure vanilla extract

10 tablespoons Apple Crisp Crust,
page 184

Vanilla Crème Anglaise

Preheat oven to 325 degrees.
Place the pie shells on a baking tray
and set aside. In a medium mixing
bowl, combine the strawberries,
blueberries, raspberries, Grand
Marnier, brown sugar, corn starch,
cinnamon and vanilla and gently
toss to combine. Divide filling
among the shells and top each pie
with 1 tablespoon of the Apple
Crisp Crust. Bake pies for 25-30
minutes. Remove and allow to cool
slightly before serving with the
Vanilla Crème Anglaise.

In a small sauce pan, add the heavy
cream, split and scrape the vanilla
bean into the cream and bring both
to a simmer over medium heat. In a
small mixing bowl, beat the egg
yolks with the sugar until pale and
creamy. Temper the egg yolk and
sugar mixture with a little bit of the
hot cream. Whisk the cream and
egg mixture into the rest of the hot
cream and cook over medium heat,
stirring constantly until slightly
thickened. Do not bring mixture to
a boil. Stain mixture through a fine
sieve and place in the refrigerator to
chill fully before using.

Red Velvet Cake page 200

the lounge

Johnny Apple Seed Burger

Barbecue Prime Beef Sliders

Barbecue Prime Beef "Sliders"

MAKES 18 SLIDERS

2 tablespoons olive oil

½ cup yellow onion, sliced

2 pounds beef chuck, cut into 1" cubes

1 tablespoon garlic, minced

1 bay leaf

2 teaspoons cumin

2 teaspoons Blackened Spice, page 178

1 tablespoon kosher salt

2 quarts water

¾ cup Southern Comfort Peach Barbecue Sauce, page 44

18 3" mini "slider buns", split and toasted

12 ounces Bleu Cheese Cole Slaw, page 156

In a small sauce pan, sauté the onions in the olive oil, over medium heat, until a light golden brown. Increase heat to high, add the beef and continue to cook until the meat is browned on all sides. Add the garlic, bay leaf, cumin, Blackened Spice, salt and the water. Bring to a boil, reduce heat to a simmer, and cook until meat is tender and easily shredded, about 1 hour. Strain out meat, discarding cooking liquid. Shred meat and place back into the sauce pan. Add the barbecue sauce and heat until hot. Divide the barbecued meat on the bottoms of the slider buns and top each evenly with the Bleu Cheese Cole Slaw. Place the tops on the sliders and secure with a toothpick or small skewer.

Charred Jalapeño Pesto

MAKES 1 CUP

2 fresh jalapeños, large

1 bunch cilantro leaves and upper stems

1 teaspoon garlic, minced

1 tablespoon almond slices, toasted

½ teaspoon kosher salt

¼ teaspoon black pepper

⅓ cup extra virgin olive oil

Preheat grill to high or, using a gas burner, char the jalapeños evenly on all sides. Set aside to cool to room temperature, cut off the stems and place in a food processor with the cilantro, garlic, almonds and salt and pepper. Puree mixture on high until smooth. With the motor running, slowly drizzle in the olive oil until fully incorporated. Store in a tightly covered container and refrigerate until needed.

Chicken, Mushroom and Smoked Gouda Flatbread

MAKES 1 SERVING

1 pre-made flatbread, about 6"x 8"

1 teaspoon olive oil

6 tablespoons Basic Tomato-Basil Sauce, page 28

¼ pound cooked chicken, shredded

¼ pound Roasted Mushrooms, page 164

¼ pound smoked Gouda cheese, shredded

1 teaspoon fresh chives, chopped

Preheat oven to 400 degrees. Lightly brush the entire surface of the flatbread with the olive oil and toast directly on the oven rack for 3-4 minutes until a very light brown. Remove from the oven and cover evenly with the tomato sauce, shredded chicken meat, roasted mushrooms and the smoked Gouda. Place back on the rack in the oven for 5-6 more minutes until crust is crispy and cheese is melted. Cut into bite-sized pieces and sprinkle with the chopped chives.

Barbecue Prime Beef "Sliders" page 204

Chicken, Mushroom and Smoked Gouda Flatbread page 204

"Devil in Blue Jeans" Burger

MAKES 1 SERVING

1 10-ounce Burger Patty Mix, page 210

Steak Seasoning, page 180

2 tablespoons Southern Comfort Peach Barbecue Sauce, page 44

2 tablespoons Charred Jalapeño Pesto, page 204

2 ounces smoked Gouda cheese, shredded

1 potato burger bun, toasted

Crispy Fried Onions, page 100

Kosher Pickles

Preheat grill to high. Season burger patty liberally with the Steak Seasoning and grill until about half way cooked. Top burger with the barbecue sauce, jalapeño pesto and the Gouda cheese. Lower cover on the grill for 2 minutes until cheese is fully melted. Remove from the grill and place on the bun. Top with the Crispy Fried Onions and serve with lots of pickles.

Johnny Apple Seed Burger with Smoked Cheddar

MAKES 1 SERVING

1 10-ounce Burger Patty Mix, page 210

Steak Seasoning, page 180

Apple-Dijon Spread

2-3 slices red onion

2 ounces smoked Cheddar cheese, shredded

¼ apple, julienned

1 potato burger bun, toasted

Kosher pickles

Preheat grill to high. Season burger patty liberally with the Steak Seasoning and grill until about half way cooked. Top burger with the Apple-Dijon spread, sliced red onion and the smoked Cheddar cheese. Lower cover on the grill for 2 minutes until cheese is fully melted. Remove from the grill, top with the julienned apples and place on the bun. Serve with lots of pickles.

Apple-Dijon Spread

2 tablespoons Apple Butter, page 34

1 tablespoon mayonnaise

1 tablespoon Dijon mustard

Combine all ingredients.

Napa Valley Burger with Red Onion Jam

MAKES 1 SERVING

1 10-ounce Burger Patty Mix, page 210

Steak Seasoning, page 180

3 tablespoons Red Onion Jam, page 30

1 ounce Boursin cheese

¼ cup Thyme Marinated Tomato Salad, page 210

1 potato burger bun, toasted

Kosher pickles

Preheat grill to high. Season burger patty liberally with the Steak Seasoning and grill until about half way cooked. Top burger with the Red Onion Jam and the Boursin cheese. Lower cover on the grill for 2 minutes until cheese is fully melted. Remove from the grill and place on the bun. Top with the Thyme Marinated Tomato Salad. Serve with lots of pickles.

"Devil in Blue Jeans" Burger page 207

Napa Valley Burger with Red Onion Jam page 207

Shrimp, Artichoke and Pesto Flatbread

MAKES 1 SERVING

1 pre-made flatbread, about 6"x 8"

1 teaspoon extra virgin olive oil

3 tablespoons basil pesto

¼ pound small shrimp, cooked and rough chopped

¼ pound frozen artichoke hearts, thawed

2 ounces fresh goat cheese, crumbled

½ teaspoon crushed red pepper

1 teaspoon Balsamic Syrup, page 142

1 teaspoon fresh chives, chopped

Preheat oven to 400 degrees. Lightly brush the entire surface of the flatbread with the olive oil and toast directly on the oven rack for 3-4 minutes, until a very light brown. Remove from the oven and cover evenly with the basil pesto, shrimp, artichoke hearts, goat cheese and crushed red pepper. Place back on the rack in the oven for 5-6 more minutes until crust is crispy and cheese is melted. Cut into bite-sized pieces, drizzle with the Balsamic Syrup and sprinkle with the chopped chives.

Thyme Marinated Tomato Salad

MAKES 1 CUP

1 cup grape tomatoes, split in half

1 tablespoon extra virgin olive oil

1 teaspoon red wine vinegar

1 tablespoon red onion, minced

1 teaspoon fresh garlic, chopped

1 teaspoon fresh chives, chopped

1 teaspoon fresh thyme, chopped

Pinch sugar

Kosher salt

Black pepper

In a small mixing bowl, toss the tomatoes with the olive oil, vinegar, red onion, garlic, chives, thyme and sugar. Season with salt and pepper and allow to sit at room temperature for 30 minutes to allow flavors to develop.

Triple Prime Burger Patty Mix

MAKES 8 SERVINGS

2½ pounds course ground chuck

1¼ pounds course ground brisket

1¼ pounds course ground sirloin

1 tablespoon sea salt

1 teaspoon black pepper

Combine all of the ingredients in a mixing bowl and very gently mix just until well combined. Be careful to not over mix the meat. Weigh the meat into 10-ounce balls and gently flatten into 1" thick discs. Do not compress too tightly. Put patties on a parchment paper lined tray and place in the refrigerator for 30 minutes to set before grilling.

If you prefer to grind your own burger meat there are a few important things to remember.

#1 Place your grinding equipment in the freezer for a few hours before grinding. Cut the meats into 1" cubes and toss with the seasonings. Using a large die, pass the meat through the grinder twice.

#2 It is not necessarily the type of meat, but rather the ratio of fat to meat and the size of the grind that makes a great burger. As long as you have a good ratio of fat, about 25%, pass it through a large grind die twice and you keep the meat cold through the grinding process, your burgers will have great taste, texture and juiciness.

Shrimp, Artichoke and Pesto Flatbread page 210

Wedding Events

celebrations

Wedding Events

Cocktail and
Hors d'oeuvre
Receptions

Intimate,
Holiday and
Corporate Events

celebrations

A Warm Welcome

Eddie Merlot's offers several private and semi-private dining areas, giving you a variety of choices to meet your needs, with accommodations available for as few as ten guests or as many as 300. In addition, our entire restaurant is also available for large corporate or charitable functions.

People love to come to Eddie Merlot's for special events. That's because we have great food, but also because we take care of everything. We'll help you greet your guests, hang up their coats and even valet park their cars. And when it's all said and done, we'll clean up– leaving you just as relaxed as your guests.

Eddie Merlot's has earned its reputation by serving exceptional U.S.D.A. Prime beef- a superior certification awarded to only 2% of all U.S. beef. And we bring the same standard to our private dining menus, which feature a wide variety of hors d'oeuvres, entrees, desserts, and accompaniments, complimented by the finest wine and cocktails. From the moment your guests arrive, Eddie Merlot's talented culinary team is dedicated to providing you and your guests with an experience like no other.

That same commitment extends to our service staff. We pride ourselves on hospitality, from making you feel comfortable during the planning process to making your guests feel welcome when they're with you. It's an experience guaranteed to please your guests.

Whether you're entertaining colleagues, clients, family or friends, our staff is dedicated to helping you make your event truly special.

Wedding Events

Barbecue Spiced Bacon Wrapped Scallops

25 fresh diver scallops, 10/20 sized

2 tablespoons Brown Sugar BBQ Rub, page 178

25 slices bacon

25 tooth picks

Fresh jalapeño slices (optional)

Preheat oven to 400 degrees. Toss the scallops with the barbecue rub to evenly coat and set aside. Lay the bacon flat on a baking pan and place in the oven for 3-4 minutes until soft. Remove bacon from the oven. Wrap each slice of blanched bacon around each scallop, securing with a toothpick. Place skewers back on the baking pan. Increase oven temperature to 425 degrees. If using, top each scallop with a jalapeño slice. Bake scallops for 8-10 minutes until just barely cooked through.

Crab Lettuce Wraps with Mustard Sauce

MAKES 20 SERVINGS

20 bibb lettuce leaves

1 pound jumbo lump crabmeat

2 tablespoons Smooth Mustard Sauce, page 44

10 grape tomatoes split in half

1 tablespoons fresh chives, minced

Wash and dry bibb leaves and line on a serving platter. Divide the crabmeat evenly between all the cups. Spoon about a half teaspoon of the mustard sauce over each cup. Top each with a grape tomato half and sprinkle with chives.

Rosemary Mustard Beef Skewers

MAKES 20 SERVINGS

20 pieces prime beef tips, cut into 1 ounce strips

1 tablespoon olive oil

2 teaspoons Dijon mustard

1 teaspoon whole grain mustard

1 teaspoon fresh rosemary, minced

Kosher salt

Black pepper

20 6" wooden skewers

Preheat oven to 350 degrees. In a mixing bowl, toss the beef tips, olive oil, mustards, rosemary and salt and pepper until thoroughly coated. Thread each beef strip onto a skewer. Place the skewers on a baking sheet and cook in the oven until golden brown and still pink inside, about 8-10 minutes.

This is a very simple and creative finger food to put together for an informal gathering. You don't even have to put them together if you don't feel like it, you could leave everything in little bowls and let your guests build their own.

Rosemary Mustard Beef Skewers page 218

Seafood Medley

Spicy Oyster "Shooters" with Fresh Horseradish

MAKES 20 SERVINGS

20 shot glasses

1½ cups Eddie's Cocktail Sauce, page 34

20 fresh small oysters, shucked

1 cup high quality vodka

10 teaspoons fresh horseradish, grated

Lemon wedges

Saltine crackers

Line the shot glasses on a serving try and fill each with 1 heaping tablespoon of cocktail sauce. Place one shucked oyster into each shot glass. Top each oyster with a little over 2 teaspoons vodka followed by ½ teaspoon of horseradish. Serve with the lemon wedges and crackers.

Spinach and Artichoke Bruschetta

MAKES 25 PIECES

1 loaf French style bread

Olive oil

Kosher salt

Black pepper

1 batch Spinach and Artichoke Dip, page 74

2 cups Cheddar cheese, shredded

Fresh parsley, chopped

Preheat oven to 350 degrees. Cut the bread on the biased, about ½" thick until you have 25 pieces. Brush each slice liberally with olive oil and season lightly with salt and pepper. Toast in the oven until lightly toasted, about 6 minutes. Divide the Spinach and Artichoke Dip evenly on top of each piece of toast and sprinkle with the Cheddar cheese. Return to the oven for 10 minutes until dip is warm and the cheese if fully melted. Transfer to a serving platter and sprinkle with the chopped parsley.

Warm Roasted Olives with Peppadew Peppers

MAKES 8 CUPS

6 cups assorted whole olives

1 cup whole almonds

10 whole garlic cloves, peeled

1 cup peppadew peppers, cut in half

1 tablespoon Herbs de Provence

1 tablespoon crushed red pepper

10 fresh thyme sprigs

4 fresh rosemary sprigs

2 oranges, quartered

1 cup extra virgin olive oil

½ cup red wine vinegar

Preheat oven to 325 degrees. Toss all of the ingredients together in a mixing bowl and transfer to a large baking dish. Cover with aluminum foil and bake in the oven for 1½ hours. Remove from the oven and remove the oranges, thyme and rosemary. Serve while still warm.

Warm Roasted Olives with Peppadew Peppers page 222

Nickel & Nick

Artisanal Cheese & Fruit

Berry White Martini

MAKES 1 SERVING

1 ounce Smirnoff Strawberry Vodka

1 ounce Smirnoff Raspberry Vodka

¾ ounce Triple Sec

Splash Sweet and Sour

Raspberries

Blueberries

Place the first 4 ingredients into a shaker with ice. Shake well and strain into a chilled martini glass. Garnish with fresh raspberries and blueberries.

Blueberry Lemon Drop

MAKES 1 SERVING

2 ounces Smirnoff Blueberry Vodka

1 ounce fresh lemon juice

½ ounce simple syrup

¼ ounce Blueberry Monin Syrup

5 fresh blueberries

Place the first 3 ingredients into a shaker with ice. Shake well and strain into a chilled martini glass. Pour the blueberry syrup down the center for a layered effect, and garnish with fresh blueberries.

Crunch Berry Cocktail

MAKES 1 SERVING

1½ ounces Smirnoff Raspberry Vodka

1½ ounces Dekuyper Buttershot

Splash Dekuyper Luscious Raspberry Rush

Splash Nocello Walnut

Caramel Sauce, page 192

Cap'n Crunch cereal, crushed

Place the first 4 ingredients into a shaker with ice. Shake well and strain into a martini glass rimmed with Caramel Sauce and Cap'n Crunch cereal.

French Martini

MAKES 1 SERVING

1½ ounces Absolut Raspberry Vodka

¾ ounce Chambord

½ ounce pineapple juice

¾ ounce cranberry juice

Fresh raspberries

Place the first 4 ingredients into a shaker with ice. Shake well and strain into a chilled martini glass. Garnish with fresh raspberries.

Berry White Martini page 226

Georgia Peach Kiss

MAKES 1 SERVING

1½ ounces Southern Comfort

1½ ounces Absolut Peach Vodka

Splash cranberry juice

Splash simple syrup

2 frozen peach slices

Place the first 4 ingredients into a shaker with ice. Shake well and strain into a glass with the frozen peaches.

Mangotini

MAKES 1 SERVING

1½ ounces Absolut Mango Vodka

½ ounce Peach Schnapps

½ ounce pineapple juice

½ ounce Sweet and Sour

Splash sparkling wine

Place the first 4 ingredients into a shaker with ice. Shake well and strain into a chilled martini glass rimmed with sugar. Top with the sparkling wine.

Mochatini

MAKES 1 SERVING

1½ ounces Vanilla Vodka

¾ ounce coffee liqueur

¾ ounce dark Crème de Cacao

½ ounce heavy cream

Coffee beans

Place the first 4 ingredients into a shaker with ice. Shake well and strain into a chilled martini glass. Garnish with coffee beans.

Pineapple Jalapeño Martini

MAKES 1 SERVING

Pineapple wedge, rind removed

2 jalapeño slices, seeds removed

2½ ounces Smirnoff Vodka

Splash pineapple juice

Muddle pineapple wedge and jalapeño in a mixing tin. Pour in vodka and pineapple juice. Add ice and shake well. Pour into a chilled martini glass. Garnish with a pineapple wedge and jalapeño slice.

Mangotini page 228

Pineapple Upside Down

MAKES 1 SERVING

Splash grenadine

1 Maraschino cherry

2½ ounces Vanilla Vodka

½ ounce Liquor 43

2 ounces pineapple juice

Place the grenadine and cherry into the bottom of a chilled martini glass. Combine the rest of the ingredients into a shaker with ice. Shake well and strain into the martini glass.

Pomegranate Martini

MAKES 1 SERVING

1 ounce Smirnoff Raspberry

1 ounce Pama Pomegranate Liqueur

½ ounce Sweet and Sour

Pomegranate seeds

Place the first 3 ingredients into a shaker with ice. Shake well and pour into a chilled martini glass. Garnish with pomegranate seeds.

Smores Cocktail

MAKES 1 SERVING

1 ounce Vanilla Vodka

1 ounce Godiva Dark

1 ounce Half & Half

Marshmallow Fluff

Graham cracker crumbs

Place the first 3 ingredients into a shaker with ice. Shake well and strain into a glass rimmed with Marshmallow Fluff and graham cracker crumbs.

White Italian Cocktail

MAKES 1 SERVING

1 ounce Dumante Verdenoce

1 ounce vodka

½ ounce Kahlua

1½ ounces Half & Half

Caramel Sauce, page 192

Crushed pistachios

Place the first 4 ingredients into a shaker with ice. Shake well and strain into a glass rimmed with Caramel Sauce and crushed pistachios.

Pomegranate Martini page 230

Holidays

We also have a very popular option that only comes along once a year: lunch. We start lunch on the Monday following Thanksgiving and offer our last lunchtime availability on December 23. We can host your business lunches as well as special work events and parties during daytime hours, giving us more availability that helps us accommodate all of our guests.

source guide

Black Wing Quality Meats
www.blackwing.com
All things elk, filets, strips, ribeyes, racks, flank steaks and roasts

Cedar Plank .Com
www.cedarplank.com
Cooking planks of all sizes and different types of wood, even flavored planks

D'Artagnan
www.dartagnan.com
All natural and organic food products from around the world

Eddie Merlots
www.eddiemerlots.com
USDA Prime steaks, burgers and seasonings delivered to your door

Gourmet Food Store
www.gourmetfoodstore.com
Anything truffle related, winter/summer truffles, oils, butters, juice and sauces

Hula Girl Foods
www.hulagirlfoods.com
All types of sugar cane products from batons and skewers to swizzle sticks and chopsticks

K – Paul's
www.chefpaul.com
Andouille sausage and tasso ham

Maple Leaf Farms
www.mapleleaffarms.com
Midwest duck products, breasts, whole duck and confit

Minors
www.soupbase.com
Every soup mix and base you can think of

Pearson Ranch
www.pearsonranch.com
Fresh California Meyer lemons, oranges, pomelos, and orange blossom honey

Salt Works
www.saltworks.us
Different types of gourmet sea salts from around the world.

Very Asia .com
www.veryasia.com
Sriracha chile sauce, fish sauce, sweet soy sauce, Chinese sausage

Wild Idea Buffalo Company
www.wildideabuffalo.com
Wide selection of grass fed buffalo products, from steaks and roasts to brats and jerky.

index

A

A Really Good Tartare Sauce, 26
Ahi Tuna Wonton Tartare Sauce, 60
Ahi Tuna Wontons with Tartare Sauce, 60
Almond Breading, 146
Andouille Sausage and Shrimp Stuffed Quail, 130
Andouille Sausage and Shrimp Stuffing, 130
Andouille Sausage Gravy, 26
Apple and Peach Crisp, 184
Apple Crisp Crust, 184
Apple-Dijon Spread, 207
Apple Spice Cake, 184
Applewood Bacon Brittle, 184
Asparagus and Potato "Risotto", 156

B

Bacon and Gorgonzola Cheese Crust, 26
Bacon Lettuce and Tomato Salad, 92
Bacon Wrapped Barbecued Shrimp, 60
Baked Brie En Croute with Cherry Jam, 62
Baked Macaroni and Cheese, 156
Balsamic Herb Vinaigrette Dressing, 92
Balsamic Syrup, 142
Banana Cream Pie, 186
Banana Pastry Cream, 186
Bananas Foster, 188
Barbecue Glazed Cedar Plank Salmon, 138
Barbecue Prime Beef "Sliders", 204
Barbecue Spiced Bacon Wrapped Scallops, 218
Barbecue Spiced Duck Breasts, 130
Basic Tomato – Basil Sauce, 28
Beef Bourguignon over Buttered Noodles, 114
Beef Carpaccio with Arugula Salad, 62
Beef Stock, 52
Beefsteak Tomato and Onion Salad, 92
Berry White Martini, 226
Bibb Salad with Champagne Vinaigrette, 94
Black and Bleu Beef Bruschetta, 62
Black Truffle and Lobster Risotto, 138
Blackberry Cobbler, 188
Blackened Prime Steak Salad, 94
Blackened Scallops with Bleu Cheese Sauce, 138
Blackened Spice, 178
Black-eyed Pea and Corn Relish, 132
Bleu Cheese Butter, 172
Bleu Cheese Cole Slaw, 156
Bleu Cheese Potato Chips, 64
Blueberry Jalapeño Barbecue Sauce, 28
Blueberry Lemon Drop, 226
Bourbon and Brown Sugar Brine, 54
Bourbon-Jalapeño Creamed Corn, 158
Bourbon Marinated Pork Chops, 114
Bourbon Marinated Ribeye Steak, 114
Bourbon Pecan Toffee Pie, 188
Boursin Cheese Butter, 172

Braised Beef Short Ribs, 116
Braised Pork Osso Bucco, 116
Brie Cheese and Honey Icing, 186
Brown Sugar BBQ Rub, 178
Brussels Sprouts with Bacon and Parmesan, 158
Burgundy Wine Sauce, 28
Buttermilk Fried Lobster, 64

C

Caesar Salad Croutons, 94
Caesar Salad Dressing, 96
Caesar Salad with Homemade Croutons, 94
Cajun Seasoned Ribeye Marinade, 54
Calamari Batter, 66
Campfire Chicken and Lime Soup, 78
Campfire S'mores Tart, 190
Candied Bacon, 96
Candied Pecans, 96
Caramel Macchiato Cake, 190
Caramel Sauce, 192
Caramelized Red Onion Jam, 30
Caribbean Jerk Spice, 178
Carrot Cake, 192
Champagne Vinaigrette, 96
Charred Jalapeño Pesto, 204
Chef Matt's Meatballs, 64
Cherry Duck and Goat Cheese Tart, 68
Cherry Jam, 68
Chicken, Mushroom Smoked Gouda Flatbread, 204
Chicken Rub, 180
Chicken Stock, 52
Chilled Fresh Strawberry Soup, 78
Chimichurri Pork Chops with Pineapple Salsa, 116
Chimichurri Sauce, 30
Chipotle Butter, 172
Chipotle Grilling Sauce, 30
Chocolate Pots de Crème, 192
Christmas Mud Pie, 194
Cinnamon and Clove Spiced Moroccan Ketchup, 32
Cipollini Onions and Charred Jalapeño, 158
Citrus Semifreddo, 194
Clarified Butter, 172
Classic Crème Brulee, 194
Coconut Cream Pie, 196
Coffee Crusted Lamb with Mint Pesto, 118
Coffee Rub, 180
Corn and Duck Confit Ravioli, 132
Crab and Corn Chowder, 78
Crab Cocktail with Mustard Sauce, 66
Crab Lettuce Wraps with Mustard Sauce, 218
Crab Louie Salad, 98
Crab Louie Salad Dressing, 98
Crab Pasta Salad with Spinach and Artichokes, 98
Crab Stuffed Portobello Mushrooms, 66
Cream Cheese Frosting, 196

Cream of Broccoli with Three Cheeses, 80
Cream of Mushroom with Sherry Wine, 80
Creamed Corn with Leeks, 160
Creamed Horseradish Sauce, 32
Creamed Spinach Steak House Style, 160
Creamy French Dressing, 100
Creamy Wasabi Sauce, 32
Crème Brulee French Toast, 196
Crispy Fried Onions, 100
Crispy Fried Sesame Calamari, 66
Crunch Berry Cocktail, 226

D

"Devil in Blue Jeans" Burger, 207
Dijon Elk Chop with Fennel Mushroom Sauce, 118
Duck Filling for Goat Cheese Tart, 68

E

Eddie Merlot's Chopped Salad, 100
Eddie Merlot's Creamy Herb Dressing, 102
Eddie's Bread Seasoning, 180
Eddie's Classic Grilled Filet Mignon, 118
Eddie's Crab and Bleu Cheese Stuffed Shrimp, 140
Eddie's Famous Shrimp Cocktail, 68
Eddie's Garlic Mashed Potatoes, 160
Eddie's Homemade Apple Butter, 34
Eddie's Homemade Mayonnaise, 34
Eddie's Potatoes, 160
Eddie's Shrimp Cocktail Sauce, 34

F

Filet and Lobster Wellington, 120
Filet Trio of Medallions, 120
Five Cheese Mac'n'Cheese Sauce, 36
Florida Stone Crab Claws, 70
French Martini, 226
French Onion Soup, 82
Fresh Horseradish and Herb Crust, 140
Fresh Horseradish and Herb Crusted Walleye, 140

G

Garlic and Herb Chicken Brine, 54
Garlic-Ginger Dipping Sauce, 36
Garlic Honey Mustard Vinaigrette, 102
Georgia Peach Kiss, 228
Goat Cheese Stuffing, 136
Gooey Fudge Sauce, 198
Grilled Ahi Tuna Steaks with Spicy Mustard Sauce, 140
Grilled BBQ Chicken with Black-eyed Pea Relish, 132
Grilled Bison Filet, 120
Grilled Cajun Ribeye, 122
Grilled Chipotle Beef Skewers, 122
Grilled Herbed Chicken Marinade, 56
Grilled Scallop Ceviche, 70
Grilled Veal Chop Dijonnaise, 122

H

Hash Brown Casserole, 162
Hash Brown Potatoes, 162
Herbed Brown Butter, 174
Hoisin Barbecue Chicken Wings, 70
Hoisin Barbecue Sauce, 36
Hollandaise Sauce, 38
Homemade Worcestershire Sauce, 38

J

Johnny Apple Seed Burger with Smoked Cheddar, 207

K

Kentucky Bourbon Steak Marinade, 56
Kentucky Bourbon Sauce, 198

L

Lemon and Roasted Garlic Aioli, 38
Lobster Bisque, 82
Lobster Butter, 174
Lobster Mashed Potatoes, 162
Lobster Ravioli with Duck Confit, 142
Lobster Stock, 52
Lobster Stuffing for Ravioli, 142
Lyonnaise Potatoes, 162

M

Mangotini, 228
Maple and Apple Cider Glazed Sea Bass, 142
Maple-Cider Vinaigrette, 106
Mediterranean Style Mussels, 72
Mediterranean Vegetable Broth, 54
Merchant De Vin (Winemakers Sauce), 40
Merlot Butter, 174
Merlot Iceberg Salad, 102
Meyer Lemon Chicken, 132
Meyer Lemon Vinaigrette, 134
Mint Pesto, 118
Minted Mango Salsa, 144
Mochatini, 228
Mojito Fish Marinade, 144
Mojito Marinated Swordfish with Salsa, 144
Mustard Butter, 174
Mustard Dressing, 132

N

Napa Valley Burger with Red Onion Jam, 207
New England Clam Chowder, 84
New Orleans Mixed Grill, 124

P

Pan Fried Almond Crusted Walleye, 146
Pan Fried Crab Cakes, 72
Pan Fried Soft Shell Crab, 146
Pan Seared Duck with Shiitake Sticky Rice, 134
Peanut Brittle, 198
Peanut Butter Cup, 198
Peppercorn and Brandy Sauce, 40
Pickled Red Onions, 102
Pico de Gallo, 128
Pineapple Jalapeño Martini, 228
Pineapple Upside Down, 230
Pomegranate Martini, 230
Potato and Leek with Fresh Thyme, 84
Potato Croquettes, 164
Prime Beef and Vegetable Soup, 84

R

Ranch Salad Dressing, 104
Raspberry Sauce, 198
Red Ginger-Soy Vinaigrette, 40
Red Velvet Cake, 200
Red Wine Mignonette Sauce, 42
Red Wine Vinaigrette, 104
Roasted Beet and Goat Cheese Salad, 104
Roasted Garlic and White Bean Soup, 86
Roasted Mushrooms, 164
Roasted Tomato Soup with Parmesan and Pesto, 86
Romaine Waldorf Salad, 106
Rosemary Cheese Polenta, 164
Rosemary Mustard Beef Skewers, 218
Rosemary Mustard Glazed Chicken, 134
Rum and Honey Black Bean Salsa, 72

S

Sautéed Dover Sole, 148
Sautéed Gulf Red Snapper with Rock Shrimp, 148
Sautéed Pork Tenderloin with Red Eye Gravy, 124
Sautéed River Trout Meuniere, 148
Savory Beer Marinade, 56
Seafood Barbecue Sauce, 42
Seafood Bouillabaisse, 150
Seared Ahi Tuna with Sesame Crust, 150
Shiitake Sticky Rice, 166
Shortbread Cookies, 200
Shrimp, Artichoke and Pesto Flatbread, 210
Slow Roasted Prime Rib with au Jus, 124
Smoked Red Chili Chimichurri, 42
Smoky Succotash, 166
Smooth Mustard Sauce for Seafood, 44
Smores Cocktail, 230
Southern Comfort and Peach Barbecue Sauce, 44
Southwestern Caesar Salad Dressing, 108
Southwestern Chicken Caesar Salad, 108
Spicy Asian Style Mustard Sauce, 44
Spicy Oyster "Shooters" with Fresh Horseradish, 222
Spinach and Artichoke Bruschetta, 222
Spinach and Artichoke Dip, 74
Spinach Butter, 176

Spinach Salad Hot Bacon Dressing, 106
Spinach Salad with Hot Bacon Dressing, 106
Sriracha Chili Ketchup, 46
Steak au Poivre, 126
Steak Butter, 176
Steak Diane, 126
Steak Diane Sauce, 46
Steak House Bleu Cheese Dressing, 108
Steak Seasoning I, 180
Steak Seasoning II, 180
Steamed Mediterranean Halibut, 152
Stilton Stuffed Filet, 126
Strawberry Poppy Seed Dressing, 110
Sun-dried Tomato and Cheese Stuffed Chicken, 136
Sweet and Spicy Chili Dipping Sauce, 46
Sweet and Sour Cabbage, 166
Sweet and Spicy Rock Shrimp, 74
Sweet Ginger and Oolong Tea Marinade, 152
Sweet Ginger and Oolong Tea Marinated Cod, 152
Sweet Potato Bisque with Candied Pecans, 86
Sweet Potato Gravy with Grand Marnier, 48
Sweet Thai Chili Noodles, 168

T

Tapenade Butter, 176
Tempura Green Beans, 74
Texas Red Star Chili with Jalapeño, 88
The Best Bleu Cheese Sauce, 48
Thyme Marinated Tomato Salad, 210
Toasted Barley Risotto, 168
Tomato and Fresh Vegetable Gazpacho, 88
Tournedos Rossini, 128
Traditional Béarnaise Sauce, 48
Triple Berry Pie, 200
Triple Prime Burger Patty Mix, 210
Truffle Butter, 176
Truffled Madeira Sauce, 50
Truffled Mashed Potatoes, 168
Tuscan Grilled Panzanella Salad, 110
Tuscan Strip Steak, 128
Tuscan Tomato-Olive Relish, 128
Tuscan Turkey Salad, 110

V

Vanilla Bean Butter Sauce, 50
Vanilla Crème Anglaise, 200
Veal Mother Sauce (Basic Veal Sauce), 50
Voodoo Jerked Chicken, 136

W

Wagyu Flat Iron Steak, 128
Warm Roasted Olives with Peppadew Peppers, 222
White Italian Cocktail, 230

locations

Eddie Merlot's locations

Montgomery Rd. and I-275
10808 Montgomery Rd.
Cincinnati, Ohio 45242
513-489-1212 Phone
513-489-0103 Fax

Polaris Parkway and Lyra Drive
1570 Polaris Parkway
Columbus, Ohio 43240
614-433-7307 Phone
614-433-7103 Fax

Jefferson Pointe Shopping Ctr.
1502 Illinois Road South
Fort Wayne, IN, 46804
260 459-2222 Phone
260 459-8896 Fax

96th and Keystone
3645 E. 96th Street
Indianapolis, IN 46240
317 846-8303 Phone
317 846-8125 Fax

Corner of 4th St. and Muhammad Ali Blvd.
455 South Fourth Street, Suite 102
Louisville, KY 40202
502-584-3266 Phone

Coming Soon!

Burr Ridge, Illinois
201 Bridewell Drive
Burr Ridge, Illinois 60527

Warrenville, Illinois
28254 Diehl Rd.
Warrenville, Illinois 60555